HOW I SOLD
30,000 eBooks on
AMAZON'S KINDLE

An Easy-To-Follow
Self-Publishing Guidebook
2016 Edition

MARTIN CROSBIE

WWW.MARTINCROSBIE.COM

ISBN: 1492241504
ISBN-13: 978-1492241508

Table of Contents

Preface to the Third Edition

Although many changes have taken place since the first edition of this guidebook was published our goal has not changed. It still is to produce a professional e-book and gain a return on our investment as quickly as possible so we can spend our time writing for our readers. So, our start and end points remain the same, the route we take is the same, but some of the aids we'll utilize along the way have changed. I've altered those in this book. The websites that are most effective have been updated and the most efficient way to run a promotion has been changed. And, the tier system of published work will be discussed for the first time within these pages in a whole new chapter. As always I hope you find the information in this updated book valuable and worthy of your reading time.

Martin Crosbie

April 2016

Preface to the Second Edition

I'm asked in interviews from time to time to comment on what I think the self-publishing industry will look like or *be* like next year or the year after. My answer is always the same. The only thing that's going to be consistent is that things will continue to change. Technology will improve, e-books will look different, and the ways in which authors connect with readers will change too. Those things will continue to change. That was part of the challenge when I wrote the first edition of *How I Sold 30,000 eBooks on Amazon's Kindle - A Self-Publishing Guidebook.* The information was current when I published the book, but at any moment that could all change. And, it did.

The guide you are about to read illustrates a method of producing your book in a professional yet still cost-efficient manner. The philosophy contained herein is designed to show you how to do that honestly and ethically. When this book was released in July 2013 it enjoyed some success. I was fortunate to see it rise to bestseller status in its category and sell several thousand copies within a short period of time. That initial success waned slightly, but the book continued to sell quite well. At the end of 2013 it was my top seller and was selling more copies than the novel that had done so well for me, *My Temporary Life*. I was receiving five-star reviews and emails from authors thanking me for outlining my methods. The only problem was that areas of the book had become less relevant. The major concern I had was that free promotions, especially through Amazon's KDP Select program, weren't as effective as they once had been. And other, different methods of selling books and connecting with readers were beginning to work. Plus, several new websites had appeared, and it looked like they were going to give some serious competition to the tried and true sites. So, I had a book that was dated in a couple of areas. The basic philosophy was the same. The process that an author should follow to produce a book that can stand spine to virtual spine with traditionally published books didn't change either. And, both of these areas probably will never change. But, the marketing strategies needed to be altered.

In December of 2013 I rewrote several sections of the book and updated the *Helpful Links* section at the back. I republished the book, added *2014 Edition* to the title, contacted Amazon, and asked them to alert previous e-book buyers that the content had been updated. They were kind enough to do this. Everyone who had already purchased the e-book was able to go to the "Manage My Kindle" tab and receive a book that was current. This got me thinking. Six months down the line I was potentially going to be faced with the same challenge. So, why not continually update the book? Why not attempt to make the content the most current of any self-publishing guide on the market? That is the book you're about to read.

I was proud to read reviews stating my guide was more specific than some that "led you down the garden path," as one reviewer claimed. Although you may find this read to be inspirational (and I certainly hope you do), my purpose is to show you specifically where to find the best editors, cover designers, and beta readers. I want to show you where to find review sites, and most importantly, promotional sites. The basic shell of the book is the same, but the specific strategies and outlets where you'll find help have been tried, tested, and updated to make your journey easier than mine and those of my colleagues. Technically this is the third edition, but the previous changes were minor compared to those included in this edition. This is a front-to-back revision with careful consideration given to making sure the entire content is current. I'll continue to update and keep you aware of changes and opportunities, so please accept the newer e-book copies as you're alerted from Amazon. My goal is to update the content every twelve to eighteen months. Good luck, and I hope you find the information within these pages worthy of your reading time.

Martin Crosbie
February 2015

INTRODUCTION

This is the book I didn't want to write. I saw the books that promised to tell you how you could make thousands of dollars a month when you self-publish your e-book and offer it on Amazon's Kindle, and I saw the books that promised sure-fire success at becoming a bestselling Indie author. I didn't want to be that guy. I felt I had the qualifications to help other authors. I'd gone from being rejected one hundred and thirty times by traditional publishing to hitting the top five on Amazon's overall bestseller list with my self-published book, and creating a steady stream of monthly income from my writing. I knew how to get there; I just didn't want to write a book about it. All of that changed when I attended a self-publishing fair in March 2013. The fair was organized by a writers federation. I'm a reluctant member of the organization. I always think about the Groucho Marx line. He says something along the lines of "I'd never belong to any club that would have me as a member." So I pay my dues every year, read their newsletters, and ignore everything they do. This time I didn't though. It was a *self-publishing* fair and I'm a self-published, or Indie, author. So I went. And I left there angry, very angry.

There was a fantastic turnout. It was an all-day event and approximately one hundred authors attended; some were published and some weren't, and most of them stayed all day. They wanted to know how to publish their own books, and the information given to them was incorrect. They were told that they need to hire outside firms to assist in marketing, social networking, distribution, and product placement. They were told about all the expenses they were going to incur in order to publish their book. And they were told that they can't succeed with only one book. They were told all the things that CAN'T be done. The organizers of the fair were wrong though. The things they said CAN'T be done CAN be done, and I know this because I've done them, and I do them every day. So I made a decision to try to get the word out there myself, and that's why I wrote this book.

The purpose of this project is two-fold. First of all, I want to show you how you can do almost all the things necessary to publish your own work, yes, *self-publish*, by yourself, without paying outside companies to help you. After all, that's what SELF-publishing is all about. And, secondly, I'm going to introduce you to a different way of thinking. I'm going to teach you how to approach your writing career as though you're running a small business, and in doing that, I'll show you how to run it-again, by yourself-and have promotional and sales opportunities come to you. I'm going to do it in a slightly different format though. This book is set up as part workbook/part guide, so that you can do the work, chapter by chapter, and evaluate your progress in the following section. I don't want you to read this book and not follow through. I want you to produce the best work you can, publish your book, and find readers. First though, I'll give you my credentials, because you need to know whether I know what I'm talking about.

When I hit my early forties I started a checklist of goals I wanted to accomplish. One of those goals was to write a book. I was the guy in grade school and high school who wrote stories and had the teacher read them to the class. I loved writing fiction. Unfortunately, in my grown-up career, I didn't pursue any type of creative endeavor. I became a sales trainer/manager for a recreational vehicle dealership. So, when I felt that I'd accumulated enough grey hair, I began to make some changes. I took up long-distance running, I started taking better care of myself, and I decided I wanted to try to write a book. I signed up for creative writing classes, and over the next couple of years, I learned and relearned the art of writing.

This is a course that never ends. I attended a writers conference a few years ago, and I listened in on a panel of bestselling authors. The one thing they all said during their speeches was that they were trying to become better writers. As I sat in on their presentation I came to the conclusion that if authors who have sold millions of books are trying to become better writers, you bet I'm going to keep trying to get better at my craft also. So, I took some classes, and because of a very encouraging instructor, I completed the first draft of the novel that would become *My Temporary Life*. Then, when the classes ended, I joined a writers group. Two years and several rewrites and revisions later, thanks to input and critiques from the group, I had a novel that I thought was pretty good. I wanted to make sure though.

I'd been sequestered with the writers from my group, and I needed some impartial input. I handed it out to friends and family members. Their comments were all positive. I thought my work was done, but my sensible younger sister had a slightly different take on it. She loved my book but wondered if I was getting legitimate criticism; all of the readers I'd given my book to knew me. She wondered if perhaps they were so impressed that I had written something, anything, that they just wanted to continue to encourage me.

With my sister's help we handed out my manuscript to friends of hers who didn't know me. These were my first beta readers, and we'll talk more about beta readers in Chapter Two. Again, all the comments that came back from the impartial readers were very positive. In fact, almost all of them asked if there were any more books by the same author because they'd like to read more. At that point, I thought I had a pretty good book on my hands.

That's when I started to send *My Temporary Life* out to publishers and agents. This is called the querying process, and it's something that, because of my self-publishing success, I'll hopefully never have to do again. I'm not suggesting that you shouldn't pursue this avenue; in fact, we'll compare traditional to self-publishing throughout this book, and you can decide for yourself.

Most literary agents and publishers have different sets of parameters in terms of how they want to be approached. Some of them want authors to submit only a synopsis of their work, others want the first ten pages, and some want the first three chapters. Plus they all have slightly different requests when it comes to how they want the material sent to them. Writing a query letter and a synopsis was almost as hard as writing my novel, and I discovered I wasn't very good at it. I sent out over one hundred and thirty query letters. I had less than one hundred responses. I sent out so many queries that I needed a way to track them all. I used Query Tracker: **www.querytracker.net**. They have an excellent program that will help you keep your queries organized and show you updated information on the more active literary agents and publishers. And their basic program is free.

Some of the folks I corresponded with wanted to read more of my work, and some weren't interested at all. In the end, none of the agents wanted to try to sell my novel to a publisher, and none of the publishers wanted to publish my book. After eighteen months of trying to find an agent or a publisher, I had a manuscript that readers kept telling me they enjoyed but nobody was willing to take a chance on. I was stuck.

While I was sending out my work and querying, I was trying to learn more about publishing in general and how it worked. During that time I discovered there was a quiet, little revolution taking place. The walls were coming down, and some innovative authors had found a way to reach readers without going through the traditional gatekeepers (agents and publishers). They were self-publishing. Initially, I thought self-publishing was a vanity-type endeavor for authors who couldn't get traditionally published (like myself). I was half right. There are hybrid-publishers that will charge authors money to publish their work, but there are also authors publishing their work by themselves for other reasons. One of them is to maintain control of their work. There are other reasons too, and hopefully they'll become clear to you as we progress through the work in this book.

My opinion of self-publishing being a vanity project was wrong, so wrong. I realized this when I started looking at and reading self-published books. My education into the self-publishing industry began where a lot of things begin these days—on Facebook. Yes, Facebook. I started making friend requests on Facebook to authors who had self-published. I knew they were self-published authors by reading their author profiles, or bios, on Amazon.com. We're going to talk a lot about Amazon because according to most statistics, 65% of all e-books sold are sold by Amazon, and that's where I've been successful. And we're going to talk primarily about e-books and e-book sales because, although I've sold a fair number of print books, and continue to do so, I've sold tens of thousands of e-books. That's where the real reading/publishing revolution is taking place.

When I "friended" authors, I'd send them a message through their Facebook profiles, congratulate them on their success, and mention that I'd purchased their e-books. I wanted to know more about what was happening in self-publishing, and I believe that to be successful in any field, you learn from surrounding yourself with successful people. To my astonishment, the vast majority of authors I contacted accepted my friendship and messaged me back. Sometimes it was with encouragement, other times they suggested which Facebook groups I should join that might help me, and sometimes they'd even ask me about my own novel. This was the beginning of building my support group. This is an extremely important part of the process in terms of building your small business, because, although we're authors first, we're self-published, or self-employed, and we need to approach this as though we're running a small business.

Because of the information I learned from these authors, and because no one wanted to publish my work traditionally, I decided to self-publish my novel. So, in December 2011, I pushed the "upload" button and became a published author. I still didn't have the confidence to *call* myself an author, but that was about to change very quickly.

Due to a number of different factors, and luck was certainly one of them, in February of 2012 the book I wrote in the spare bedroom of my house, that over one hundred and thirty agents and publishers didn't want, hit Amazon's top ten overall bestseller list and stayed there for a week. It hopped over traditionally published books like *The Hunger Games* and the *Twilight* series. I sold about eighteen thousand e-books that month. And I made $46,000. It was a very, very surreal time. I totally felt as though I was living someone else's life.

Because of my success all kinds of things began to happen. Amazon mentioned me in a couple of press releases; in fact, later on, in their year-end release they called me one of their "2012 Success Stories." *Publisher's Weekly* gave me a mention, *Forbes* online magazine interviewed me,

Canada's second largest newspaper, *The Globe and Mail*, ran a full-page article on me in their weekend edition, and other media outlets from all over the world reported on my self-publishing journey. To date, **My Temporary Life**, the book that's been so good to me, has been downloaded as a paid e-book over thirty thousand times, and I've given it away over two hundred thousand times. The "giving it away" part requires further explanation, and in Chapter Nine, I will explain exactly how free promotions work and how to effectively utilize them.

I've self-published the sequel to my first book now too, as well as a collection of short stories, a romance novel, and a thriller that was published by Kindle Press, an Amazon imprint (more about this in the final chapter). All are selling well, and I've been really fortunate to have gained an extremely supportive group of readers who follow my career. And some months I'm able to support myself as a writer, something I'd only dreamed of doing previously. So I'm a very lucky guy. The self-publishing fair I attended told authors in the audience that you can't do what I've done, and they said you certainly can't do it with one book. I'm here to show you that you can. And I'm going to show you how.

Can it be done again? Yes, it can. Many authors have self-published their work and sold countless more books than I have. Do you need some luck, a good or even a great book, plus all the tools that are in this book? Yes, you do. I sell books every single day, and I have my ear closer to the ground than most Indie authors. There are no secrets; there is simply a process and a change in thinking if you are going to succeed as a small business owner/Indie author, because that's what you are. You have a business that you can run any way you desire. If you follow the steps I'm going to outline, and you have a book that readers want to read, you can do it too.

For those of you who have already self-published, you may only pick up a handful of techniques from this book, but those techniques might just be enough to help you gain some momentum and find new readers. And, for those of you who have not hit the "upload" button yet, this will show you how it worked for me. Although I will talk about some of the things that did not work, this book is about what you CAN do. And finally, this book will tell you what you need to know without resorting to tech-speak. All you need is some basic computer knowledge, and you'll be able to follow along easily. This is not a one hundred percent guaranteed method of turning your book into a bestseller or finding thousands of readers, but it will make sure you produce and present a professional product that you'll be proud of. So, if you're ready, let's get to work.

CHAPTER ONE
CREATING YOUR PROFILE
Or
It All Began with My Close, Personal Friend—Sir Anthony Hopkins

For a short period of time, Sir Anthony Hopkins, the actor who played Hannibal Lecter, as well as many other memorable roles, was my friend. Unfortunately, it ended a couple of years ago when he had the audacity to "unfriend" me on Facebook. Up until that time we had a fantastic relationship. I "liked" many of his posts, congratulated him when he celebrated his birthday, and I friended many of his friends. Then, for some reason, he chose to abandon our friendship. Fortunately, I was able to recover.

I love Facebook. As most of you know, it's a free website where you can interact and become friends with folks you may never otherwise have the opportunity to meet. I joined Facebook several years ago but only began seriously developing my online profile, or personality, shortly after I completed the final draft of *My Temporary Life*. Up until that time, I didn't really participate, but when my book was finished, and especially when I was getting nowhere in terms of being traditionally published, I jumped in and tried to meet more people.

Around that time, as I continued to research self-publishing, I read a blog by Joe Konrath and an article by Seth Godin. Seth wrote a book and gave it away for free several years ago. Then, he built up enough momentum that he went on to sell thousands of books afterward. Joe Konrath did it too. Joe is one of the original big guns in the Indie author movement. He gave away his book through Amazon and afterward hit several bestseller charts. And he was, and still is, extremely generous in terms of sharing his findings with the rest of us through his blog posts and articles. You can find more information on Joe here: **jakonrath.blogspot.ca/.** *By the way, all of the links that are spread throughout this book are included in the Helpful Links section at the end of the book.*

As I read Joe's blog posts, I discovered he wasn't only talking about giving his e-book away but also about a way to circumvent the *gatekeepers* and a new way to connect with readers. I needed to know this information because as I said, I was receiving rejection notices from agents and publishers almost daily. The letters lined the walls of my office. I actually ran out of room and started putting them on my fridge and kitchen walls. I used them to motivate me. I wanted to be reminded that I had something to prove. It got to the point that if I didn't wake up to an emailed rejection letter I felt as though something was missing from my day.

My book takes place in North America as well as the United Kingdom, so I queried agents all over the world, and subsequently, I was rejected by agents from all over the world. It was becoming very clear that if I was going to get my work out to readers, other than the group of beta readers who had enjoyed *My Temporary Life*, I needed to do something different. I kept thinking that if I could just get my book out there, to a large group of people, the world would recognize my brilliance and all kinds of opportunities would follow. I felt that maybe then the traditional publishing world would notice me, a movie deal would appear shortly thereafter, and I'd be able to concentrate on writing full time. It was a great dream but I was wrong about one thing. In the self-publishing world that I was about to jump into, and, to some extent, in the traditionally published world also, you can't sit back and wait for the world to recognize your brilliance. You need to do the work in order to find readers.

There are exceptions to this rule, but unfortunately, I wasn't one of them. One of the most notable exceptions is Hugh Howey. Hugh wrote a novella in the summer of 2011 and self-published it through Amazon. Initially, he did almost no social networking or promoting yet his short book, *Wool,* took off. Readers emailed and messaged him asking for more, and word spread like wildfire. Today, *Wool* is a five-part omnibus and a consistently huge seller. Hugh has sold the print rights in a six-figure deal but retained the digital (e-book) rights. Paramount bought the movie rights from him and lined up big-time producer, Ridley Scott, to create the film version. He's written several other books too and in an interview, when referring to his Amazon royalty checks, he said, "Most of my months are six-figure months."

Hugh found lots and lots of readers for his self-published work with minimal initial promotion; he's one of the exceptions though, and he climbed the bestseller rankings based almost solely on one thing: content. He wrote a very, very good book and readers discovered it and told each other about it. Since then Hugh has become more prolific at social networking and interacting with readers and other authors, and like Joe Konrath, he shares his progress with the rest of us. Hugh's website is here: **www.hughhowey.com/.**

Other authors have had similar success with minimal online interaction, but most found their readers through extensive social networking. Russell Blake and Amanda Hocking had books that readers enjoyed, and one of the ways they found their market was through Facebook and Twitter. Russell's site is here: **russellblake.com/.** And Amanda's blog is here: **hockingbooks.com/blog/.**

Although I felt I had a good book, I wasn't going to be one of the exceptions. I would find out, shortly after I self-published, that my book needed some help in order to find an audience, and it wasn't going to take off on its own. So it was fortunate, at this point, before I published, that I was building an online identity. I started researching Indie, or self-published, authors. I searched them out on Amazon's website, read their author pages, requested their friendship on Facebook, and started following them on Twitter. I wasn't picky, either. I wanted to be a successful author, so I made a "friend request," or in the case of Twitter, followed traditional authors also. Surprisingly enough, a lot of them, especially the Indie authors, accepted my friendship, and some followed me back. That's when I noticed one of the authors who had become my friend was also a friend of Sir Anthony's, so after a request from me, I became online friends with the great actor himself (for a little while).

As you build your circle of friends and acquaintances online, there are several things you need to be aware of. Yes, there are rules.

1. **What you say, and how you say it, is who you are.** Be aware that every move you make online indicates the type of person you are.

2. **Be careful who you get close to.** Build your support system with others who are on the same path as you.

3. **Join the groups that will help you succeed.**

4. **Don't get thrown into Facebook jail or banned from Twitter.** If you friend request too many folks you don't know, Facebook will temporarily suspend your privileges, and if you're tweeting your tweeter off, Twitter will shut you down for a little while.

5. **Limit the intrusions you make on others.** Too many Facebook events, Tweets that are blatant spams, and automated direct messages can result in people tuning you out.

6. **Pick your networks and find a balance.** The majority of your time should be spent writing, not marketing online, so decide which social networks you're going to participate in.

1. What You Say Is Who You Are

Just like in real life, the only thing I really have is my name, and yes, it's the same name that's on the cover of my books. Remember, other than smiley faces and clever little graphics, the only thing that identifies you online and determines who you are is your words. When you tell me what political party is the "right" party for the country, or you give me your opinion on who's going to win the Super Bowl, or mention emphatically that all people who eat aged cheddar should be tortured at midday in the town square, I'm going to form an opinion of you. Yes, you might post exceptionally attractive pictures of yourself too, but I'm going to define you based largely on what you say because that's what we do. So when you offer your opinions, and we all do this, it's important to remember to do it courteously and politely.

I interact on Facebook, Twitter, and LinkedIn to find readers for my books and to build my support system. I'm a lucky guy; I have lots of friends already, away from the online world, but I like people, and I'm always happy to make more friends. I've formed some incredibly close friendships with folks I've met online and that's a great thing, but my primary purpose when I'm on Facebook or Twitter (or especially, on LinkedIn) is to introduce myself to people who may be interested in reading my books. I want to put my best foot forward, and I want you to think of me as the polite, courteous, nice guy that I believe I am. So I'm careful. If there's something I believe in I'll stand up for it, but I always remember that there are potentially hundreds, or maybe even thousands, when I calculate the "friends of friends" factor, who may be watching what I say.

As you show the world who you are and build your online identity, be careful how you say what you say, and remember that when you offer your opinion, always approach people in a respectful and considerate manner. You may not realize it but you are a brand, and you're building that brand. It's very important to create and build it realizing that the final product is a reflection of who you are. In other words, forget that you're online. Practice the same manners when you're typing that you would if you were face to face with someone.

2. Be Careful Who You Get Close To

This is very important. When you start interacting online, you're going to have the opportunity to virtually "meet" other authors—lots of them. There are some who are working at building a career but will become discouraged and give up. Others approach the online world in an unethical or less than honest manner and try to manipulate the system. Others, like you, are working hard to build their reader base and become better writers, and their ultimate goal is to write full time. Obviously, it's this last group of writers you want to align yourself with.

In my support group, I have authors who are on the same path as I am. We share everything with each other and enjoy the camaraderie of reaching up, trying to climb to that next tier of success. I'd go to the wall for these writers. They're good at what they do, they subscribe to the "pay it forward" philosophy, and I know they're going to be successful. Some of them write in the same genres as I, and others are writing totally different material. This is important too. I want to know what's going on with science fiction even though I'll probably never write in that genre. It's important for me to know what's trending, or what's hot, no matter what kind of story it is.

Because of my relationship with my core support group, I have access to their beta readers, their cover designers, their editors and formatters, and most importantly, we share the results of our promotions with each other. Instead of spending lots of money advertising everywhere, we pool our information and determine which sites are most effective in promoting our work.

In terms of how you determine who you should be close to, think of it this way. You want to have colleagues who are going to tell you the truth. Early in my self-publishing journey, I forwarded my Amazon product page and a copy of my book to a prominent self-published author. He'd had huge success with his book, and I wanted to mine his knowledge. He was brave enough to tell me the truth. He told me that I had a "crappy synopsis" and my cover was not indicative of my story. He had some other hints too, and I made all of the changes he suggested. Throughout this book, I'll pass along his suggestions to you. He was kind enough, and again, brave enough, to tell me the truth. Needless to say, he's still in my support group, and he's exactly the type of confidante you should be seeking out.

Don't let this part of the process worry you. If you're starting to think of this as a business and your goal is to become a full-time writer, people will fall into place and you'll find that you will indeed align yourself with others who are on the same path as you. Keep promoting the "pay it forward" philosophy within our community. By that I mean share information, help promote others' work that you believe in, and generally just help each other. You absolutely can't go wrong by doing this, and at some point you'll look around and the folks surrounding you will be on exactly the same path you are.

3. Join and Participate in the Groups/Forums That Will Help You Succeed

I belong to several writers groups on Facebook. Some are specific groups where writers share information, others are for promoting books, some help me find beta readers, and some help me find reviewers. Some of them have authors offering opinions all day long on what Amazon's next move is going to be and why, some are more of a social outlet for people who write, and others are filled with writers who totally subscribe to the "pay it forward" philosophy and are helping each other.

In February 2012 I ran my first and most successful free promotion. The idea, believe it or not, is to give away as many e-books as you can over a short period of time (specific details are in Chapter Nine). I ran my promo over three days, and early on the third day, a Sunday, I was at #2 on Amazon's overall free list. This was a heck of an accomplishment. I was very pleased with myself, and I'd had lots of help getting there. I'd used social networking, and Facebook especially, to help spread the word about my book and the fact that it was available for free. So, having been stuck at #2 for over twenty-four hours, and not thinking I could climb any higher, I posted on the many Facebook groups to which I belonged and thanked all the other members for their support in helping me spread the word. My favorite group was the MasterKoda group. This is a group of writers who always support each other. Minutes after I posted my thanks the group administrator, Kim Mutch Emerson (another author of course), rallied the troops. She said, "Guys, let's get Martin to #1. Tweet, email, Facebook, whatever you have to do, but let's get him there."

Thirty minutes later my book was the #1 most downloaded free e-book on Amazon. And it stayed there until my promo ended at midnight that night. The comments after Kim's declaration on that thread were all affirming that they'd done what they could, and were doing what they could, to spread the word. Everybody joined in, including many authors who didn't know me. There may have been other factors at play at the time. Maybe there was a backlog from Amazon's reporting system that came through all at once or maybe one of the major websites decided to feature me at that moment (although I never could confirm this), but I like to believe it was the other writers in that group who unselfishly helped my book reach over fifty thousand Kindle owners that weekend.

That was *paying it forward* and that's what can happen by being in the right support system and the right Facebook group. Previous to this incredibly generous gesture, I'd helped lots of other writers in the MasterKoda group and other groups too, and I like to think that's how I was paid back. Even though I was a rookie writer at the time, if any of the group members had questions, I tried to answer them. I took time to help wherever I could because I'd had lots of help myself.

Join the Facebook groups where the members are paying it forward and succeeding and where they're taking responsibility for their successes and failures. Not everything I've done in terms of promotion has worked. When it hasn't succeeded, I haven't blamed anyone but myself, and I've tried to adjust my strategy so that it doesn't happen again. I want to have colleagues and belong to groups where writers are paying it forward, taking responsibility for their actions, and succeeding. Yes, Amazon is going to make business decisions that are detrimental to my sales strategies from time to time, but they have much better things to do than sit around plotting how they can mess with Indie authors. Again, I believe that in order to succeed and excel, I need to surround myself with successful people, and that's whom I try to associate with.

Facebook and LinkedIn have search capabilities where you can find writers groups. Use the search terms "Indie Writers," "Self-Published Writers," or try "E-books." By doing this you'll find groups where you will eventually promote your work and groups where you'll find folks on the same path you are. And, in a short period of time, by participating in the groups and reading the threads you'll be able to determine if it's the right group for you.

4. Don't Get Thrown in Facebook Jail or Banned from Twitter

I've been suspended temporarily from Facebook six times, and although I've never had Twitter shut me down, I've had friends who have experienced this. Hopefully, I've learned my lesson and I'll never be in jail again. I attribute this to the learning curve that I've been on since I started interacting online. I'll share my findings with you so that hopefully you can avoid jail time.

Facebook has guidelines, and if you cross those lines they may temporarily suspend you from sending messages to people you don't know and making friend requests for periods from five to thirty days, or in rare instances even longer. And their ultimate threat is to permanently ban you from their site. When you friend request someone you don't know, Facebook will occasionally ask that person whether they know you from somewhere other than Facebook. If too many of these potential friends say they don't know you, and they refuse your requests, Facebook may put you in jail. In order to avoid this, it's best to only approach folks whom you know from a common Facebook group, or have a large number of mutual friends with, or if you've made it very obvious that you're both in the same field.

For example, in my description on my main page, or wall, I spell it out that I'm an Indie author and mention my book titles. Then, if I contact another author, it's pretty obvious that we're in the same field. I'll also contact book reviewers (and we'll talk about how to do this and where to find them in Chapter Six), and occasionally I'll friend request potential readers. This can be tricky. If someone has listed on their profile that they are an avid reader, you may want to send a polite message and ask if he or she would like to be your friend, as you're an avid reader too, (all authors seem to be), and you're also an author. This goes back to my first point: always approach potential friends, or readers, in a polite and courteous manner. Once your book is out there and you've had readers enjoy it, you'll have folks approaching you and requesting your friendship, but for now, tread carefully and you'll be able to stay out of jail.

The interaction you have with others on Twitter is much different from

Facebook. Although there is a "Direct Message" or "DM" aspect to its site by which you can send messages to your followers, the majority of your interaction will be from sharing your thoughts in one hundred and forty characters or less, and by reading others' thoughts and sharing them or "retweeting" them from time to time. If your Twitter feed becomes promotion after promotion, especially if it's for the same book or product, and you do it consistently within a short period of time, Twitter will temporarily shut you down. Or, if you "churn,"—follow and then "unfollow" other users in order to build your numbers up—Twitter also may suspend your account.

It's a tricky balance. We want to interact with people and talk about our work without crossing the line. I've had followers who have been so aggressively promoting one of my books that Twitter has suspended them. Be careful—mix up your promotional tweets with information that your followers might be interested in. Nobody wants to watch commercials all day long, and it's important that sites like Twitter and Facebook don't become one long advertisement. That's why these safeguards are there. And limit the people you follow (and especially unfollow) each day. Work within the rules and you'll have no problems.

5. Limit the Intrusions You Make on Others

This is part two of my previous point. There are a number of ways to promote your work using Twitter and especially Facebook. Be careful how frequently you use them and *how* you use them. I routinely receive two or three invites a week to Facebook events, and when I look at the main feed on Twitter, the majority of the posts are "buy my book" type entries. Plus, when I follow new people on Twitter, quite often they will direct-message me and immediately ask me to check out their book. And most of those messages are generated from an automated system; it's not even the user sending them to you. This isn't how sales works, and it certainly isn't how relationships should be developed either. Here's an article I wrote for Indies Unlimited detailing the correct way to approach new friends online: **www.indiesunlimited.com/2013/03/07/buylike-my-bookpagewebsite/**

In sales, you'd never walk up to a potential customer and immediately try to close the deal. You build the relationship and qualify the person by trying to see if they may indeed be interested in your book or product, and then, at the appropriate time, ask whether they might be interested in knowing more about your work. On my main Twitter page, I have a brief description of what I do, and again, I mention my books. When I have a new follower, I don't immediately ask them to "like" my Facebook page or buy my book. If I buy a book I'll share it on my Twitter feed, and if there's a promotion for a book I believe in, I'll share that also, but in between these promotional efforts I'll share other things too. I enjoy inspirational sayings, and if I find one that's working for me I'll tweet it. Or if there's an article that pertains to something I'm interested in, I'll share that too. Or if I want some feedback from readers and other authors on a potential book cover or synopsis that I'm working on, I'll tweet it. I do however, limit the pictures that I post or tweet. Although this can boost your visibility, I think if you post them too often followers will tune you out. They might see your picture or post, but if it's the same old thing that you post all the time, their minds won't even register it, and after a while they'll drop you from their lists.

In Facebook, you can create and hold an event. You can use these for book launches, or, if you have a book signing or promotion, you can send invitations to your friends. Like Amazon, Facebook is a sophisticated, ever-changing entity. The way you interact with your friends and how many of your friends actually have the ability to see your posts changes as Facebook alters its settings. It's estimated that, with their current settings, if you post an announcement about the release of your book, approximately six percent of the people on your friend list actually see it. And if you host an event, you can only invite one hundred friends at a time until there are a pre-set number of invites accepted (this may change in the future). This is different from posting a Facebook ad, and we'll talk about ads and their effectiveness in Chapter Nine. If this all sounds confusing, that's because it is, and it's changing all the time.

The safest approach is to only run a Facebook event if you have a major announcement such as a book release or major promotion. And limit them to two or three events a year. The only exception to this would be if you have an online radio show and want to inform your listeners of the weekly lineup. Other than that, they can become very irritating and a sure-fire way to lose friends and potential new readers. Bear in mind, you need to keep your Facebook settings to "public" so that potentially, if the Facebook masters allow it, your friends' friends can also see your postings. As you accumulate friends, you're not just interacting with them, you're also potentially interacting with their contacts and friends also. This is why, once again, it's important to respect the rules and work within them and not let your page or Twitter feed become a constant barrage of promotions.

6. Pick Your Networks and Find a Balance

You have some choices to make. There's Facebook, Twitter, LinkedIn, Google+, Pinterest, StumbleUpon, Tumblr, and a multitude of other social networks out there. Plus there are Yahoo Groups and forums like Kboards, Amazon author discussions, and KDP Community forums. I don't have time to participate in all of them and neither do you. You and I should be writing. We have to supply product to our readers. To find new readers, maintain the reader connections we have, and more importantly, in order to become better writers, we need to be writing. Not promoting. There, I said it out loud; now I just have to follow my own advice and do it.

It's far too easy to spend time trying to find the social network that will help us discover a gazillion new readers. This is especially true if you've written a book that has done quite well and want to push it to the next level. It's important to do that, but we just don't have time to *only* do that. We need to work at our craft and satisfy our readers. Currently, I have the original version of my bestselling novel, ***My Temporary Life***, available for sale as well as five other books, I occasionally teach workshops or speak at events, and I have several other projects in development. These are all worthy tasks and fantastic opportunities, but at the same time, I should be producing more work, different work. Fortunately, I'm doing that too. I'm writing the revised version of this book, I'm working on the next novel in my "John Drake" series, and I work frequently on the third installment of the *My Temporary Life* trilogy. And, while this is all happening, I only participate in the social networks that work for me.

Early on, I went through a phase where I joined every network where other authors were having some success, I joined several forums and participated in the comments section, and I put together a website and posted a blog. This was a great learning experience. It gave me information on so many different aspects of the self-publishing industry, but at the same time—I wasn't writing. So, now, I have a schedule. I participate in Facebook daily, Twitter two to three times a week, LinkedIn once a week, (or when I have an announcement to make). I update my blog and post it on my website, StumbleUpon, and Blogger. I occasionally check in on Kboards, Amazon author discussions, and KDP Community forums. And I participate on Goodreads two to three times a month. We'll talk more about these sites and discussion-type groups when we learn about promoting your work in Chapter Nine. Those sites are my choices because I'm familiar with them, and they've been effective for me in terms of finding readers. How do I know that? I've tested it, many times. I ask new readers who email me where they found my work. In doing this I know what works for me.

Investigate what's working, quiz your support group, especially the writers who write in the same genre as you, and decide where you're going to focus your efforts. You can't do everything. And limit the time you spend online. I know of a hard-working, bestselling author who sends her modem to school with her kids. She actually packs it into one of their schoolbags, so that while they're at school she can't connect to the Internet. That way, she can write during the day and then connect online when the kids get home. This is an extreme and, for us, quite humorous measure, and hopefully you don't have to resort to this. Pick where you're going to participate and limit the time you spend there—find your balance. When we reach Chapter Twelve we'll expand on this, and I'll show you a method for finding and maintaining your balance. I think you'll find it helpful.

CHAPTER ONE HOMEWORK

1. Search out the blogs or websites of authors who can help you. Read their latest entries and save them under the "Favorites"

section on your computer.

2. Start building a support group and join some writers groups. Determine whom you want in your core group and who will be on the periphery by finding out who will really tell you the truth. Find the groups that work for you—the ones that have the same goals you have.

3. Pick which social networks are best for you, participate in them in a respectful and courteous manner, and build your friends/followers list.

4. Develop and maintain a schedule of which sites you're going to frequent, how long you're going to be there, and how often. Find and maintain a healthy balance between promoting, looking for new opportunities, and most importantly—writing.

CHAPTER TWO
CONTENT
Or
How I Came to Hate NaNoWriMo

I hate NaNoWriMo. Really, I do. For those of you who don't know what NaNoWriMo is I'll explain. NaNoWriMo is National Novel Writing Month. It's a writing challenge that takes place in November each year. Over a thirty-day period, writers write a novel. That means writing thousands of words each day. It's a fantastic way to discipline yourself as a writer. My friend, Indie author Bruce Blake, always tells me, "Writers write daily." He's right. We should and lots of us do.

The problem with NaNoWriMo is that some authors produce a first draft in thirty days and then self-publish it. There's no in-between time. It's a great accomplishment to produce fifty or sixty or one hundred thousand words in the period of a month, but when you're finished, I don't believe you have a novel, or at least I know I couldn't produce a completed work in that amount of time. I believe you have a first draft. So by all means use NaNoWriMo as a challenge. It's a great way to network with other writers who are serious, and of course a way to get your work started, but please don't consider it as a way to complete your book, because it isn't. Ernest Hemingway said, "The first draft of anything is shit." I tend to agree.

Here's NaNoWriMo's website address:

www.NaNoWriMo.org/.

Have a great November, but once you've completed, remember, that's only step one. Here's the step-by-step guide I use to get my content ready for publication.

1. **Writers Groups**
2. **Beta Readers**
3. **Editors**
4. **Proofreaders (beta readers)**
5. **Editors (optional)**

1. Writers Groups

I wrote the first draft of my first novel during a creative writing class. I handed the work in to the instructor each week and he patiently critiqued it. I had the opportunity to take advantage of his expertise, so I worked diligently before each class, getting more words on the paper (or screen, actually), and handed it in to him, for I knew that once the class ended I might not have the benefit of his feedback. At the end of the six-week course, I had a pretty good start on my book, and the instructor was kind enough to continue sending me feedback when I forwarded him my weekly output. From there, once I'd written my book and thought I'd finished telling my story, I had nowhere to go. Luckily, I was invited to join a writers group. This was a stroke of luck. Writers groups are a great way to get feedback on your work from others who have either been where you're going or are on the same path.

You can find lists of local writers groups in your community by doing a Google search. It's important to determine the type of group you need before sitting in on a meeting or asking for an invite. I've found that I can go online to learn about promoting my work and the state of the self-publishing industry and interact with other self-published authors. I don't need to take time out to physically meet with them.

There are different types of writers groups. In some the primary purpose is to talk about how to get published, and others are more of a critique group. And there are some who do a bit of both. The group I joined was a critique group. At the time, I didn't know the difference, so I got lucky. My book and I needed to be part of a critique group. The other members of the group included traditionally published authors and some who were unpublished, like myself. Some gave a line-by-line critique and others wrote down very little but would give an overall opinion of how my work made them feel. It was all helpful, and it was exactly what I needed at the time.

When I joined the group, one of the first things I said was that I had completed my novel. None of the members disagreed with me. But, over the course of the coming weeks, it became clear that my work wasn't complete and the group was aware of that. I was probably on my third or fourth draft when I joined the group, and during my time there, *My Temporary Life* would go through several more rewrites and revisions. And, along the way, the group helped me clean up some of my pesky editing issues. This was invaluable and certainly helped me save money when I hired an editor later in the process. I owe a lot to the Rainwriters group from Surrey, Canada. After all those rewrites and revisions, which took almost two years, I thought the story was told, and my book was ready for the world. Again, I was wrong.

2. Beta Readers

At this point I began to let the folks around me in on my secret and told them that I'd written a book. As I mentioned in the Introduction, this was how I discovered my first beta readers. Originally they were my sister's friends. They didn't know me, and when they read my work, they were asked to be especially critical. This is what you want. You want to find as many errors as possible during this first step because the next step—editing—will cost you money. So, if you can catch errors now, in the beta stage, it'll save you money later. And I'll tell you a secret. Beta readers don't charge you for reading. Or the ones I use don't. They love finding new authors and new books. Beta readers are exceptional people. They put hours into helping you make your book the best it can be. If they believe in your project, they'll later become valuable because they're going to review your book too, and that's one of the key things you're going to need in order to implement a successful marketing plan.

So how do you find beta readers? As you begin to change your thinking and truly look at the fact that you're not only an author now but also a publisher, you'll experience a shift in the way you approach situations. You'll begin to discover opportunities, and you'll find that beta readers are available to you from all kinds of places. Most people you bump into and associate with in your daily life read books, and most of them enjoy talking about the books they've read. Many of your workmates and associates have friends who don't know you. Use this to your advantage. Make bound copies of your book and have a friend or associate hand them out to their friends. Or, if your potential beta readers would rather read on their Kindle e-reader or from their computer, send an electronic copy to your mutual friend and have them forward it. By the way, everyone who owns a Kindle has a unique Kindle email address. You can email your Word document as an attachment directly to a device. Once they've read your book ask for honest feedback. And remember, the key is to make sure the beta readers do not know the author's identity.

When writing my first book, I kept thinking that if I could just get the words on the page the world would recognize my brilliance. Someone, somehow, would come along and realize that my work had to be shared with the rest of the world. This didn't and doesn't happen. If you're like me, you're going to have to change your thinking and realize that although writing a book is a monumental achievement, you still have work to do. You have to think of yourself as a publisher as well as a writer. So, as a publisher, you should always be on the lookout for opportunities, and if you keep your mind open, beta readers, or at least a way to seek out betas, will appear in your path. And if that fails, you can always go back to Facebook.

I mentioned earlier that my education in self-publishing began with Facebook of all places. Today I interact with my readers on Facebook more than any other platform. I'm very accessible, and readers find me and leave comments on my Facebook page on a regular basis. You can also find beta readers through Facebook. There are a number of different Facebook groups that are populated by readers and authors. I just did a random search on Facebook for beta readers and found these groups: Beta Readers Here, Beta Readers Wanted, Beta Readers Inc., and Beta Readers.

Some of these are closed groups. This does not mean they won't accept new members. Each group has a different set of membership requirements. You can read the requirements in the "About" section at the top of each of their pages. Most of them require that you ask to join the group. Typically, they'll ask that you list a short synopsis of your work, and then a beta will contact you. Bear in mind that Facebook groups change from time to time, but if you use the search term "beta readers" or "betas" or "book readers" and you approach the group and group members in a courteous and polite manner, as discussed in the previous chapter, you will find readers who will give you honest critiques. I've found the best approach, especially if you find the group rules are unclear, is to send a message to the facilitator of the group and tell them that you're an author looking for some honest criticism of your work. Then, ask whether they can help you, and how they'd suggest you post a request in the group. Facilitators or group founders will appreciate the fact that you're interested in respecting the group's boundaries and rules and will usually be willing to help.

Let me tell you a story about how important beta readers were to a book I wrote. Toward the end of 2013 I wrote a romance novel. I'd had a number of friends publish Christmas romances the previous year, and most of them had sold a lot of books. I was sure I could do the same. So, I spent a few months writing and rewriting a book that eventually became *Believing Again: A Tale of Two Christmases*. I now had in my hands what I considered to be a traditional romance, and I was eager to tackle that lucrative market. I'm fortunate enough to have a very good friend who is an ultra-successful romance/erotica novelist. She offered me the use of her team of beta readers. She has twenty betas who read her traditional romances. I jumped at the opportunity, of course. Because she's a well-established author, she's able to lay some groundwork with her team. She gives them seven days to complete and report back. I was on tenterhooks for a week.

At the end of the week I received notes from her betas. They didn't think my book worked. They were expecting to read a traditional romance, and they felt I hadn't achieved this. There was no clear hero, and the happily ever after conclusion (or HEA as they referred to it) was unfulfilling. Fortunately, none of them criticized my writing, but they almost unanimously declared that if they purchased this book, they'd review it unfavorably because it wasn't what they'd been led to believe. Although I was disappointed that I hadn't achieved my goal, I was over the moon with the information they'd provided me. Those readers gave me advice that would have cost thousands of dollars to procure. And, some of them even said they liked the story. They just didn't agree that it was a traditional romance.

So, I made some changes. I changed some, but not all, of the areas they recommended. This is where I listened to the little voice in my head a couple of times. In making my revisions I discovered that my muse would not allow me to write a traditional romance. I wasn't sure exactly what type of book I was writing, but according to the experts—the readers who read this genre—it did not qualify as a traditional romance. Once I made my changes I submitted my work to a new group of beta readers. I found twelve others who were interested in checking out my work. These were different readers from the first group. I found them through readers groups on Facebook, and they were all unknown to me. Fortunately, this group enjoyed the revised story and did not have the same concerns the previous group had with the draft I sent them.

After several revisions and thirty-two pairs of eyes examining my story, I had a completed product that was ready for my editor. I released my book in early December 2013, and it sold very well throughout the holidays and hit #1 in Holiday Romances. Then, a funny thing happened. My Christmas romance continued to sell well in January. In February I ran a Valentine sale on my book and sold over a thousand copies. And, it continues to sell. From the research I've done, I've determined that seasonal, especially Christmas, stories sell consistently throughout the year and peak—wait for it—not at Christmas, but during the summer. So, my little book that was vetted so thoroughly sells copies most days. And, if I hadn't had the support of all those talented beta readers, I would have released a book that may have been reviewed poorly (because readers felt I'd misled them), and I probably would not have written another one. To date it's one of my highest-reviewed books, and I may turn it into a series.

Thank goodness for the hard work that those beta readers performed in helping me become a better writer.

I was fortunate to have so much help and find all those readers, but it's not always easy. Be aware, as you're searching out beta readers, you'll come across companies that will charge you "reading fees" to read or review your work. Pass on this. There are some legitimate companies offering this service, but it's definitely not necessary to spend the money to have your work critiqued. Again, the majority of your work as a publisher, and that's the hat we're currently wearing, by the way, is going to be done by networking without any cost to you. If at some point somebody is asking you to pay, decline the offer. And, if you'd really like to know more details on the company you've found, or has found you, check them out on Preditors and Editors **(pred-ed.com/)**, Writer Beware **(www.sfwa.org/other-resources/for-authors/writer-beware/)**, or Absolute Write **(absolutewrite.com/forums/index.php)**.

These are the best sites to help you determine who's operating a legitimate company or website and who's running a less than scrupulous organization. They have a huge list of everything from agents and publishers to contests and promotional agencies. And they update their lists regularly. Whenever you come across a company that you're going to associate with or do business with, check them out on Preditors and Editors, Writer Beware, or Absolute Write.

3. Editors

By this point you should have a revised, rewritten, critiqued, clean copy of your manuscript. You've survived family and friends, other authors, and betas; it's now time to employ a professional. You need an editor. One of the reasons I wrote this book was to show you that you can do most of the tasks involved in self-publishing by yourself, and to this point, we haven't spent any money. That's about to change. I want my book to be as clean and professional as any traditionally published book on the market. Self-published authors have a target on their backs. We found a way to connect with readers while the gatekeepers were drafting new rejection letters, and some of them are all too ready to point out the deficiencies in self-published literature. This will change. The more quality, professional, self-published books that are published, the quicker this stereotype will disappear. The target is going to be there for a while though, and I'm happy to carry it around and try to help make our industry more professional. One of the first ways to do that is to make sure you hire a professional editor.

I'll let you in on a little secret—editors aren't scary. The majority of editors I've worked with have been very good people and are exceptionally professional. They have an area of expertise and their minds work differently than mine does, and perhaps yours too. They look at the words and the story, can add or eliminate details, and generally clean up your work.

If you've followed our system, you probably will have had several people, from family and friends to writers group associates and beta readers, who have read your book and suggested changes. And, hopefully, you've implemented some of those changes. I say "some" of those changes for a reason. Ed Griffin is the author of *Prisoners of the Williwaw,* among many other fine books, and he was my creative writing teacher. One of the things Ed used to preach to our class was: "Listen to all the suggestions that I make very carefully, and once you've understood them, either make the changes or throw them out the window."

His theory was that nobody knows your story (whether it's nonfiction or fiction, there's still a story being told) better than you do. We have the voices in our heads, and if the voices are disagreeing with the suggestions, then we should sometimes follow our instincts. I'll give you an example. When I was circulating one of my later drafts of **My Temporary Life** to betas and other readers, a couple of author colleagues suggested that I had in fact two novels within one, or two different stories. They felt I should publish them as two separate novels. I disagreed, and even though the suggestions were being made by authors who had more experience than I did, I listened to the little voice in my head and released my book as one novel instead of two. To date, I have over four hundred reviews on Amazon's website with a four point four out of five average rating. Only three percent of those readers who wrote reviews mentioned that it feels

36

like they're reading two books. So I know I made the right decision. Having said that, if the majority of your betas are saying the same thing, you should make the changes, and if the suggestions are coming from an editor you should almost always make the changes, especially if it's copyediting.

There are different types of editing, and we'll try to determine what you need. By this point, you've had lots of different readers reading and commenting on your work. They may have found problems with wordy sentences, continuity, sentence structure, and other content. Plus, some of them will have found grammatical, punctuation, or spelling mistakes, and you'll have already corrected those errors. There are often arguments on what the different types of editing are, but the editors I've worked with break it down into three types: substantive editing, copyediting and proofreading.

- Substantive editing usually involves reorganizing and restructuring your manuscript. This can include shaping the plot, character development, and deleting scenes as well as other major changes. If your readers have done their job, and you've used enough of them and made the changes they suggested, this should not be necessary, but if an editor is advising that you need another rewrite, then unfortunately, you need to go back to the beginning. A substantive editor can be expensive, and at some point you need to decide whether the editor is editing or co-writing your book with you. With the help of our betas we shouldn't need this type of edit.
- Copyediting is a more basic edit. Copyediting includes finding problems with grammar, tense, sentence structure, spelling, and other punctuation errors.
- Proofreading is a final check for typos and other basic errors that may have been overlooked. In point #4 I'll offer you some help with proofreading.

Don't count exclusively on Microsoft Word or some other program to find errors in your work. These types of programs work on averages, and your sentence structure might fall outside the norm or average. You'll feel more confident, and you'll maintain that professional approach that we've talked about, if you spend the money and hire an editor.

My first editor was a retired English teacher, and I found her through a friend of a friend. I had my publisher's hat squarely on my head, because I knew I was going to self-publish, and I was always on the lookout for help and opportunities. So, when I was having dinner with a friend who worked at a local college, I asked her if she knew anyone who could help me with some editing. That's how I found the editor for my first book, and she was incredibly helpful. There were points in my book that required a light copyedit and areas that required slightly more attention. Without her invaluable assistance, my book wouldn't look the way it does.

With the first book, I employed only one editor because at that point it had been read by approximately twenty-five experienced readers and authors. Even with all those examinations, once it was uploaded and offered for sale, Amazon readers still found some errors. When you hit the upload button and put your manuscript into the system, Amazon's filters will find some, but not all, remaining errors. I've found even at that point, with all the help, professional and volunteer, there's still the possibility that something can be missed. And I'm sure you've seen traditionally published articles and books with mistakes also. The advantage with e-books is you can make changes and correct errors after you publish, and you don't have to wait for a publisher to do it because remember—you're the publisher. So, even with all that help, I still had a couple of errors, and I quickly corrected them and re-uploaded my book back into Amazon's system.

With the next books that I published, I went through the same process with test readers beforehand, but, in the interest of trying to have the cleanest, most professional product possible, I employed two editors. To this point I think all of these books are error-free. I hope.

Finding an editor can be difficult. The challenges are that you don't know what you should be paying, and you don't know who is going to do a good job. And, although I used a friend of a friend for my first book, you typically do not want an acquaintance to edit your work. You want a totally objective opinion, and you really do want them to find errors.

Pricing is difficult to estimate because an editor wants to see a sample of your work before giving you a price. I hesitate to estimate pricing for you, but in the interest of giving you something to work with, I will give you some ballpark costs. Typically, a 70,000-word book, if it's been vetted and read using our system, will cost from $500 to $1,500 for a copyedit. You may find some who charge less and some who charge more, depending on how much work is required, but this is approximately what you should be paying for a light to medium copyedit. Avoid the companies that charge $5,000. That seems to be a magic number for a lot of so-called editing services companies. I'm often contacted by authors who have had $5,000 and upward estimated from these types of companies, and perhaps they're doing something that I'm not aware of, but, again, if your work has been beta read by a number of experienced beta readers, you should not have to pay that much money. And, an editor needs to see your work to estimate the cost; my figures are merely to give you a rough idea.

By the time I was ready to hire an editor for my second book, I'd made many important connections. It was through these connections that I began to meet editors, good editors. Additionally, I referenced the huge encyclopedia of knowledge that's right in front of us. No, this time it didn't involve Facebook; it was Amazon. I checked out some of the bestselling authors on Amazon in the category where I was going to place my book and I contacted them.

I went to Amazon's website, clicked onto the "Kindle Store" and then browsed the categories until I found mine. My second book, **My Name Is Hardly**, is multi-genre, much like my first book, but it has a strong suspense/thriller element to it, so I looked there as well as in the "Men's Adventure" category. I found authors whose product pages looked professional. Then, I made sure they had lots of reviews, and that none of the reviews criticized the editing in their books. I checked their rankings to make sure they were selling books (we're going to discuss how to determine this in Chapter Six), and I asked them who had edited their books. I also contacted the hottest-selling Indie author that I could find.

At that time, right before I was set to publish my second book, Hugh Howey, author of *Wool,* was probably selling two thousand e-books every day. I wasn't. So I emailed Hugh through Facebook (yes, we're back on there again) and asked him who his editor was. I'd read *Wool* and loved it and wanted some of that success to rub off on me. Hugh was kind enough to message me back and tell me that his editors were his mother and his wife. This has since changed, and Hugh does have an editor that he recommends, but at that time all his work was in-house. I thanked him but assumed that option wasn't available, so I took the recommendations of some of the other authors I'd found on Amazon who'd messaged me back.

With their help, I now had a list of three or four editors. I also consulted with my online support group and asked whom they were using for editing. Surprisingly, some of them were bartering with other authors to have their work edited. I didn't want to do this. I'm not an editor, and if I were ever asked who my editor was, I wanted to be able to give the name of a reputable professional. I took the list of editors and wrote each of their names on a small piece of paper and pulled one out of a hat.

No, I didn't do that. I just wanted to make sure you were still paying attention. I contacted each of the editors, and asked what their rates were. And, if their prices seemed reasonable, I forwarded each of them a chapter and asked for their input and for a more precise estimate on editing my complete novel. At the end of the process I had two editors I felt comfortable with, in addition to my original editor.

I encourage you to go through this same process. Having a professional, constructive relationship with your editor is very important. Just as you can rise and fall with the help you receive from your beta readers, the same can be said with the relationship you have with your editor. The right editor won't hesitate to tell you the truth. Mine will tell the truth, and as I mentioned earlier, their minds work differently. They're supremely talented when it comes to working on my books, and I'd be lost without them.

I've included the contact info of a few editors I've worked with in the *Helpful Links* section at the end of the book. I include them to tell you that I have a fantastic working relationship with these editors. You may not. Every relationship differs, and once again, I encourage you to seek out your own using the process outlined above. With the help of your own professional editor, you'll discover that your book will reach the next level and almost be ready for publishing.

4. Proofreaders (Beta Readers)

Once your book has been edited it may still require proofreading. Numerous beta readers may have read your work, you and your editor have probably gone through it several times, but you might still not be satisfied. We don't want the reading experience interrupted for any of our potential paid customers. So, after editing I often search out new beta readers. At this point I want betas who have not read my work. As you produce books you'll find that you have beta readers who stick with you. They enjoy your books and will want to read more as you continue to create. I have a prized beta reader I send unedited work to as I write. I have others, however, whom I would not dream of sending an unedited manuscript. You'll discover what type of reader you're dealing with as you receive comments back. I tend to use two to four new beta readers to proofread. Inevitably, they find errors that my editor, myself, and all those other pairs of eyes have missed.

You'll find that beta readers, just like the writers who were in my writers group, critique differently. You can ask them to evaluate your work a certain way, but for the most part they're going to give you what they've got. Some will give you feedback on continuity. They'll tell you when your story takes a turn that doesn't appear to make sense to them and either ask why you wrote the story that way, or, in some cases, give you suggestions on how to address it. Some will give you general ideas of what they liked and what they didn't, and they'll compare your work to other books they've enjoyed and tell you whether they think you're in the same league as their favorite authors. And still others will tell you that you're writing a story that's been told too many times. Or, that you're writing for an audience that doesn't exist. Almost all of them will help you with copyediting. They'll point out your punctuation errors and spelling mistakes.

As the author, you can stare at your pages for hours, trying to find an error, but your brain won't allow you to identify it. You just can't see it.

You know where the story goes and you will automatically tune in to the next part of the plot, and you'll sometimes miss the most glaring mistakes. A good beta reader will show you where those mistakes are. Beta readers are golden, and again, just like your writing group colleagues, they'll save you money on the editing process and proofread your work too. I've used the same readers for different books, but I always bring in new readers who don't know me. I want my work to be the best it can possibly be before I publish, so the more input the better. Treat your betas well and respect their opinions. I find that if I receive comments that are contrary to how I feel about my work, I sometimes need to close the email and revisit it a day later and then decide what I'm going to do with the information. Of course, if the same comments are being made by different readers, you need to take a look at your content, and if you want to reach readers and sell your book, make the changes.

5. Editors (again)

This is an optional step. I've had two books where I've employed an editor again at this point. Use your little voice to determine whether it's necessary. In other words, follow your instinct. Bear in mind your reports from betas are not always going to arrive in a timely fashion. You may receive suggestions back after your work has been edited. And, if you utilize betas in step #4 as proofreaders, there may be other non-proofreading changes that you make. If there have been a number of changes, I go back once again and employ an editor. This should be a different editor who will look at my work with a fresh set of eyes. This does not have to be a costly experience. Make sure you let your new editor know that your work has been edited and proofread and beta read to the extreme (because it should have been) and that you only need a light edit. Unfortunately this is one further cost but don't take shortcuts. If your instinct is telling you there might be errors, even if they are few in number, hire another editor.

CHAPTER TWO HOMEWORK

1. Research local writers groups. Find a couple and ask if you can sit in on a meeting. Learn how they work and decide if you want to use a critique group to help get your book ready for publishing.

2. Find beta readers by querying your support system, joining beta groups on Facebook, and asking your acquaintances.

3. Make the changes in your manuscript so that during the next step, you only require a copyedit.

4. Find three to four editors by contacting other authors whose work you admire and again, querying your support group.

5. Submit a sample chapter to two or three editors and determine who is going to tell you the truth and help make you a better writer.

6. Once you have a list of beta readers you've worked with, categorize them and decide which part of the process is their specialty. Are they best suited to proofread after editing, or do they have the type of critical skills that you'd like to employ immediately after your first draft is complete?

CHAPTER ONE FOLLOW-UP

1. Are you following the blogs of other authors who can help you?

2. How do you feel about your support group? Will those closest to you tell you the truth about your work?

3. Are you participating in groups and networks in a respectful, courteous manner?

4. Are you following a schedule, limiting the time you spend promoting, and concentrating on writing?

CHAPTER THREE
BOOK COVERS
Or
How to Find Religion, and Lose It Again, Quickly

One of the things pointed out to me after I published the initial version of my first book was that I had a cover that was not indicative of my story. I mentioned previously that after I released my book, while I was sitting back awaiting the accolades and large royalty checks (neither of which happened at that point), I contacted several other self-published authors who were selling lots of books and asked them for advice. Many of them responded, but none of them were as helpful as Robert Bidinotto.

Robert self-published his novel, *Hunter,* in the summer of 2011. He'd written a very good book, and it was a book people wanted to read. He just couldn't find a way to reach readers. When Amazon sent out an email recommendation for *Hunter* to thousands of their customers over the Thanksgiving holiday, Robert found his readers. He sold tens of thousands of e-books and consistently sold many books afterward. Even today, *Hunter* still sits high in Amazon's rankings. So, when Robert emailed me with some suggestions, I read every word very carefully.

Now a word or two of warning. If you go through this same exercise and contact other authors, do it in a professional manner. When I sent out messages and emails to authors who were selling lots of books, I purchased their e-books. I wanted to see what readers were buying. I sometimes "gifted" them a copy of my book too. Amazon has a feature that lets you send your book (at a charge to you), to another person. Bear in mind you're going to be paid a royalty on the book, so it's the net amount (the dollar difference between what it sells for and what you're paid) that you're actually going to be out of pocket for. If I read their book and enjoyed it, I made sure to pass along my compliments in my email and to leave a review also. This, again, was part of the "paying it forward" process.

Robert paid it forward to the nth degree. He, and others, helped me not only with my cover but also with my synopsis, as well as several other elements I was missing in terms of making my product more visible and professional looking. We'll discuss all of those elements throughout the book, but here, we'll start with covers.

Covers are extremely important. I'll say it again: covers are extremely important. As self-published authors we want to produce and present the most professional product we can. I want my books to sit on the same shelves (virtual and actual) as traditionally published books and look every bit as polished as they do. Plus, the cover is the first thing potential readers see when they visit your product page. When you promote your book, you should always show your true cover (sorry, couldn't resist). There are four different methods of obtaining a cover. Let's look at each of them.

1. **Make your own.**
2. **Purchase a photo and modify to suit.**
3. **Obtain a free cover from Amazon.**
4. **Purchase a pre-designed cover or hire a cover artist.**

1. Make Your Own

I write books, and I think I'm pretty good at it. Other than that I have no artistic skills. I can't cut straight using scissors, and I certainly can't color inside the lines. So I'm not going to attempt to create my own covers. This is a risky task to undertake. I suggest you only attempt it if you are indeed a very good artist or if you know someone who's exceptionally talented at this type of work. Even then, make sure you get lots of feedback after it's done, and make sure it's all positive. If not, I wouldn't recommend this method. The litmus test, as always, is to compare your work, or in this case, your cover, to other covers that are in the top twenty bestselling list of books in your chosen genre on Amazon. Plus, Joel Friedlander has an excellent site that focuses on the best covers submitted each month. You can check out his picks for the best, most professional covers and compare yours. This is Joel's site:

www.bookdesigner.com/2011/08/monthly-ebook-cover-design-awards/

So, if you have acquired an existing image, and you think you can make your cover as professional-looking as those books that are selling hundreds or even thousands of copies each day, or look like the top covers on Joel's site, give it a shot. Here are some free sites you can utilize to create your book cover using an image you already have:

Picasa **picasa.google.com/**
Gimp **www.gimp.org/**
Get Paint **www.getpaint.net/**

2. Purchase a Photo and Modify to Suit

Before receiving guidance from my author friends, I purchased a photo from a website, added my book title and name, and uploaded my book into the system. I sold about one hundred and fifty copies of *My Temporary Life* with this original cover. My book is a coming of age story that develops into a suspense/thriller. The picture I purchased had two people holding hands. They are on a hill, walking into the distance. The sun is coming up behind them, and one of them is holding a large staff. It has a spiritual, almost religious-type feel to it. My book is not a religious/spiritual-type book, and in the story, nobody is holding a large staff. Again, I thought that if I could just get my work out there, as quickly as possible, the world would recognize my brilliance and doors would open. At the time I thought the cover unimportant. I was wrong, and I was lucky that readers purchased my book with that original cover. That's not to say this method of creating a cover can't be effective. Again, if you truly have some artistic talent when it comes to visual images, or if you know someone who is talented in this field, you might be able to do it.

If you'd like to take a crack, make sure you purchase a royalty-free picture. Below there is a link to a list of sites that offer pictures that are royalty-free or pay-per-usage. You should try to purchase a picture that is royalty-free. This enables you to buy the picture and own it, and you don't have to pay a fee every time you use it. This is very important of course.

The payment system differs from site to site also. Some of them have a straight one-time charge, but with others, you purchase credits and use the credits to buy the picture. The credits stay in your virtual account for up to a year (this may vary), and you can go back and buy other pictures using your credits. The search process to find a suitable picture is fairly similar from site to site, and you can familiarize yourself with the different systems fairly quickly.

Usually, on the main page there will be a search bar, and you can type in a description of your book's main plot. For example, you might type in "Scottish castle at night with lovers embracing and a dragon in the background." If this doesn't produce an image that works, you might try "Scottish castles, lovers, night-time." If that still doesn't get you the right picture for your cover, you could try "Castle, lovers, dark." Sooner or later, going from specific to less specific, you should find an image that's indicative of your story.

You will probably want to use one of the free photo-editing programs noted at the end of the "Make Your Own" section above to modify the image that you purchase.

A very important note of warning: make sure you own the image you're using. Don't assume that just because it's online it's free. Many pictures that you find on a Google search are copyright-protected. Some companies have departments that are dedicated to finding photos used online without authorization. When they find these illegally used photos they issue copyright infringement notices to the user. They have robots online checking out your website and blog posts too. And, even though you're a small fish in a big sea, they will issue a copyright infringement notice and demand payment. I found this out at the beginning of 2013. I had accumulated a number of photos and saved them on my computer. I found them through Google searches or during other random time spent searching the Internet. They were images I found interesting and thought I might use them at some point. One of them was a photo of a man jogging through the snow. It was a great picture, and I used it in a blog post on my website. Eight months later, I was contacted by the legal department at Getty Images. They threatened to sue me for copyright infringement and wanted $1200 for the use of their picture. I immediately pulled the picture, and sure enough there was a small Getty Images watermark in the corner of the photo. They were right; I'd used their picture without authorization and without the photographer being paid. The actual value of the picture was $500, which was very expensive for a photo. After some negotiation I paid the $500. It was an expensive lesson, and it motivated me to source out where free images are available online. Although I don't use photos for my covers, I do use them for blog posts and articles. I've put together what I believe is the most comprehensive online list of sites where you can procure free images. It's on my website **martincrosbie.com/** under *Free Photos and Lower Priced Images*. Within this list you have access to virtually hundreds of thousands of free images and photos. At the time of printing many of these sites were offering their images at no cost, but I still encourage you to double and triple-check that the image is indeed free, as sites will change their rules from time to time. And, even though there may be no cost involved, sometimes an attribution is applicable, and you'll be required to list who, what, and where. This requires reading the site's guidelines, but as I discovered from my experience with Getty Images it's worth it. Incidentally, sometime after my incident Getty began to offer a number of their photos and images for free.

3.   Obtain a Free Cover from Amazon

Free is good, and as promised at the outset of this book, there are things you can do by yourself when you're publishing your book. My first cover, as I mentioned, was a religious-type design that really didn't tell readers what my story was about. When I decided to ditch that cover, I searched through the royalty-free image sites hoping to find an image that would be suitable. I put hours and hours of effort into trying to find the perfect cover, because by this point I knew how important it was. Today, it's even more important than it was in 2011. There has been a huge increase in traditionally published books sold on the virtual shelves of Amazon's website and, thankfully, self-published authors have started producing books with very, very good covers. Unfortunately, some books out there are excellent, but readers aren't getting to the content because the covers look homemade and amateurish.

At the same time I was trying to find a new cover for my e-book, I was producing a print version of *My Temporary Life* through Amazon's print-on-demand company, CreateSpace. CreateSpace has a service where, during the creation of your print book, you can utilize its databank of covers. "Cover Creator" has thousands of covers you can use for free. Then, using its online tools, you can add your name, book title, subtitle, or other information that you want on the cover. Amazon has now expanded its "Cover Creator" tool to include e-books also. So, when you publish through KDP, or Kindle Direct Publishing (and that is indeed where we're headed), you can use this free tool to create a cover.

In a roundabout way, you've always been able to do this. I found the second cover for *My Temporary Life* using the "Cover Creator" tool on CreateSpace. I found an image I liked, played around with some colors and text and came up with something that I thought worked. It wasn't perfect, but to me, it portrayed the mood and theme of the book without showing an exact image of what the plot was about. It was certainly more contemporary than my previous religious-type cover, which again, did not show the reader what my book was about. By using "Cover Creator" I came up with a cover, and used it for the print version of my book, but I still didn't have a new cover for my e-book. So I contacted Amazon through its online contact system on CreateSpace and asked if I could use the same cover on my e-book.

CreateSpace's contact system is probably the best I've seen anywhere. You type your phone number into their contact form, and within minutes your phone rings and you're able to speak to an actual live person. I've done this many times, and it never ceases to amaze me that, in this day and age, I don't have to wait on hold; I can actually talk to someone about my problem and have my questions answered quickly. And they've always been able to help me right away. When I asked if I could use the same cover for my e-book, they immediately said yes. Now I had a cover for both versions, and it didn't cost me a thing.

This cover has been very good for me, but there is one problem with this method. Your cover is not exclusive to you. You don't own it. Anyone can go into the Cover Creator system, pick the same cover you did, use the same font and produce a cover similar to yours. I know this because it happened to me. In late 2012 several readers contacted me because a book that had the same cover as *My Temporary Life* had been released. The book had a different title, but the font was the same as my book's and the cover was exactly the same as mine. The author had utilized the free cover function of Cover Creator and used the same cover that had been so good to me. My ego would like to believe that my cover was copied because of the brilliance of my work, but chances are the author just liked the cover. She didn't do anything wrong, but this was misleading for readers who were browsing Amazon's catalog. I was in the process of releasing book two of my trilogy and needed to make sure there was some similarity between my covers. Plus, there was at least one other cover out there that was a duplicate of mine. So, I had a problem. Fortunately, the answer was where it always lies—within the expertise of my very helpful support group.

4. Purchase a Pre-Designed Cover or Hire a Cover Artist

I got really lucky. Once I'd rewritten my synopsis (which we're going to talk about next), changed my cover, properly utilized Amazon's tools, and executed a strategic marketing plan, my book took off. I found thousands of readers for my work, and I needed more content. As a follow-up, I had another book I wanted to write, one that had nothing to do with the first book. I'd had the idea for quite some time and was looking forward to proceeding, but my readers had other ideas. I was receiving emails and messages (because I was easily accessible through Facebook and Twitter, as discussed in Chapter One), almost daily, asking for more information on one of the characters from my first book. Readers wanted to hear more about Gerald "Hardly" McDougall, the teenage alcoholic who went on to join the army. So I decided to turn my first book into part one of a trilogy.

This is easy to do. I'm a self-publisher; I'm one person. I don't have to sit through endless meetings or have countless phone calls with agents and publishers trying to determine if it's the right step to take. My readers wanted it, and I thought there was another story to be told, so I did it. I altered the text on the e-book and print book copies of *My Temporary Life*, calling it "Part One of the My Temporary Life Trilogy," and I wrote a book about Hardly. I completed *My Name Is Hardly* in December of 2012, and I needed a cover. I checked out pre-made covers on a number of different websites. Joe Konrath, who I mentioned earlier, sells a lot of books, and in his articles and blogs he's always quick to compliment his cover designer, Carl Graves. Carl's website is here: **extendedimagery.com/**. He has some great covers and his pricing starts around $250. The benefit of this method is that you know he's created covers for bestselling books, and by browsing his online portfolio, you'll see covers that you may recognize.

There are other sites that offer pre-made covers and some sites that will create a cover to your specifications. This is again one of those areas in which you can use your support group and Facebook writers groups to get reviews and recommendations on cover designers.

At this point in my journey, I was getting frustrated. There was another book out there with a design very similar to mine, so I had to change my cover for book one, and I needed a cover for my second book that would blend with the first book in the trilogy. Seeking out pre-made covers wasn't working; I had to hire a designer. I did two things. I quizzed my support group and asked whom they had used, and I went back to the huge online encyclopedia—Amazon. My new book was a suspense/thriller (kind of), so I browsed the top-selling books in that genre. If there were covers I liked, I found the authors' contact info on their Amazon author page and contacted them. I congratulated them on their success (because I was only contacting authors who were selling lots of books) and asked if they'd mind sharing the information on their cover designer with me. One name kept coming up, and coincidentally it was the same name that someone in my support group had suggested.

Jun Ares is a designer who does exceptional work. His real gift, though, is reading minds. I contacted Jun, gave him a short synopsis of my first book, brief information on my second book, told him what I had in mind, including the theme I wanted to convey, and he came back with some options. That's when he read my mind. He had some killer ideas, and it didn't take long for us to decide on covers for the first and second book in the trilogy. I had both back from him within days. I hesitate to quote pricing because it always depends on the project, but I can tell you that his bill was very reasonable, and each cover came in under $300. I encourage you to find your own Jun Ares. Contact authors who write books in the same genre as yours and ask who did their cover. If you'd like to see if you can work with Jun, here's his contact info: **aresjun@gmail.com.**

I'll offer an additional hint to novelists and as always, this is based solely on my own experiences. Readers want to see people on a book cover, and a woman and a man is preferable to just a man. I don't know why this is, but it seems to be true. The romance category is a given, but check out every other category in the fiction section and you'll see the majority of the top producers have the image of a woman on the cover. Even in the suspense genre, showing a woman on your cover is a good idea. We could discuss at length why this is and whether or not it's a good idea but we won't. I stand by my opinion and I advise that, as long as you have a female main character in your book, put her on the cover.

<u>CHAPTER THREE HOMEWORK</u>

1. Create a theme for your cover. Decide what you want to say visually. Remember, you're only going to be able to touch on the basic premise or main plot, not the sub-plots.

2. Pick a method of acquiring a cover. Are you going to do your own or purchase a picture and then utilize one of the free programs to modify it? Or are you going to use Amazon's free Cover Creator program? Or are you going to query your support group and other bestselling authors to find your own cover designer?

3. Get some input. Post your cover on your Facebook groups and

Facebook page. Email it to the other authors in your support group, and compare it to other books that are selling well within your genre. Does it fit? Does it look like it belongs with the other bestselling books? If not, and you're given suggestions, take them, make the changes, and complete your cover.

4. Bookmark my list of sites that offer free photos and images **martincrosbie.com/authors-tools/**. You never know when it might come in handy.

CHAPTER TWO FOLLOW-UP

1. Have you joined a writers critique group? Are they telling you the truth, and are you making the changes needed to fine-tune your product and make it as professional as possible? If not, perhaps you need to change groups.

2. Are your beta readers giving you the feedback you need? Have you made the changes they suggested? If you're not receiving enough suggestions, perhaps you need to find additional betas.

3. Continue seeking beta readers. You're going to write other books, and you're going to need help in the future.

4. Have you found an editor you trust? Is your editor suggesting changes? Have you calmed down and realized that even masterpieces are actually drafts that have been written and rewritten many times?

CHAPTER FOUR
TITLES, SYNOPSIS, AND FORMATTING
Or
Never Sweep Anything Under the Rug

We're almost there. We're almost at the point where you will publish your book and see it available for sale online. It's very important, being that we're so close, that we don't forget to look after the little details, and we address those details in a professional manner. The following items, especially book titles and synopses, will be the window, along with your cover, through which readers will examine your book. It's imperative that you present a product that's going to appeal to potential readers. Some very, very good books currently available for sale online aren't being purchased or read because the authors have made errors in the following areas. As anxious as we are to try to get our work out there, it's important to be patient and continue in the professional manner with which we've progressed so far. Here's a list of the important details we don't want to overlook.

1. **Titles and Subtitles**
2. **Synopsis**
3. **Formatting**

1. Titles and Subtitles

The original title for ***My Temporary Life*** was *But for the Morning*. I had that title bouncing around in my head for years. Before I'd even written a word of the novel, I knew I wanted to use it. I actually have a photocopied manuscript somewhere, and it has the *But for the Morning* title on the cover page. I thought it was a clever title, and it probably is.

The problem is—it's not marketable. When you tell someone that you've written or are writing a book, they tend to ask two questions: what's it about and what's it called. Any time I told them my title they always said the same thing: "What?" That wasn't a good sign.

As my rewrites and revisions started to clarify what my final product was going to look like, a new title threw itself onto my computer screen. I Googled and searched *My Temporary Life*. I thought that somebody somewhere must have used it at some point, but fortunately it hadn't been used yet. I snapped it up. I created a Facebook page with that title and changed from my original title to the new one, and it was a wise choice. It's a title that's been very good to me, and when I changed my single book to a trilogy and called it the first book in the *My Temporary Life Trilogy* it still worked. The post-analysis confirmed my choice too.

I was interviewed on Pam Stack's *Authors on the Air* radio show after I released my second book, and we spoke about book titles. Pam gasped when I told her my original title, and then emphatically congratulated me on changing to *My Temporary Life*. Pick a title that is marketable. A good title should explain and raise questions at the same time. Really, it should. It should leave the reader with a little bit of an explanation about what the book is going to deliver, and it should also have a degree of mystery about what's between the pages.

You're going to need a book title for the cover of your book of course and to catalog your book in the system. You'll also need a title for your Amazon product page, and that's where you can include a subtitle. We're going to talk about your product page in greater detail in Chapter Seven when we learn how to utilize Amazon's tools, but we'll also touch on it briefly here. The subtitle for books in a series is the series name, but if your book is a stand-alone, you may want to consider a teaser or additional descriptive blurb or even a category name. For the book cover, we don't want to add too much text, because it's going to be shrunk to thumbnail size when it's listed among other books online. We don't want it to appear too cluttered or hard for a reader to decipher, but we can get away with a bit of additional text in order to offer your reader a little more detail.

When we upload our formatted manuscript into Amazon's system, we do it from our dashboard. During this process we'll enter a synopsis, upload our cover, and enter the title. If your book is part of a series, make sure you follow the instructions and denote it as book one or two or three in the series. This way Amazon can link the books together and make it easier for the reader to find them. This section is immediately below the subtitle section on your dashboard.

In discussing subtitles I'll once again use the example of my kind mentor, Robert Bidinotto. Robert's bestselling novel *Hunter* isn't called *Hunter*. On his book cover it's actually called *Hunter: A Thriller*. On his product page it's listed as *Hunter: A Thriller (A Dylan Hunter Thriller)*. All of the text on the product page fits onto one line and that's important, and the text on the cover is still readable even at thumbnail size. He also has text above his author name on the book cover. It reads, "The Wall Street Journal 'Top 10' Bestseller." The *Wall Street Journal* is a recognizable periodical, and he was wise to list that recognition, but if your top award is a mention as a "Dave's Picks of the Week Winner," that isn't going to attract any attention. In fact it'll most likely cause you to lose credibility. Until you start hitting the big-time lists, I wouldn't include the other, more minor accomplishments on your cover or product page.

We're going to talk about keywords in Chapter Seven and how they're linked with our titles and subtitles in an important way. When a reader types a word or phrase into Amazon's search bar, their system searches out titles, subtitles, and keywords. From the research I've done I can't find any evidence that it's searching book descriptions. So, it's important to get as many broad words or terms in your title and subtitle as possible. To call your book *The Reckoning: A Romantic, Humorous, Paranormal Vampire Thriller* would lose credibility because it's too broad and potentially misleading also. You want to use the system to widen your reach as much as possible without confusing the reader. We want to help readers find our work and make sure that it's a book they're interested in. We want to build our careers in an ethical, professional manner. Remember, the only thing we have is our name and for me, it's the same name that's listed on my books.

I've usually had a title come to me while I'm writing the work. The sole exception is the book that you're reading. I would be asked over and over again what the name of my work in progress was, and I kept saying I didn't know, but I was sure it would come to me while I was writing. It didn't though. Once it was complete I scrambled to find a title. I wanted to include some relevant keywords in the title. If someone were searching for information on self-publishing, or Amazon, or Kindle eBooks I wanted them to find my book. So, as you know, the title became *How I Sold 30,000 eBooks on Amazon's Kindle—An Easy-To-Follow Self-Publishing Guidebook*. I published the book under that title in August 2013. Then, a couple of things changed. A number of new promotional sites appeared and they were quite effective in matching up readers with books. I wanted to include them as well as several other nuggets of information in my book. So, I revised the already published manuscript and uploaded the new version into the system. Now, I had what I considered to be the most current self-publishing guidebook on the market. That got me thinking.

I wondered what would happen if I continued to revise my book from time to time. As new information appeared or strategies were developed I wanted to share them with other authors. I contacted Amazon, and they helped me with a couple of items. They allowed me to change the name of my e-book. I added *2014 Edition* to the end of my title, and more importantly, after some consideration, they notified previous buyers of my original book that there was an updated copy available for download – at no cost to them. I asked if I could continue to revise and whether they would keep alerting previous buyers, and they agreed on the condition that the information was critical to the content. Well it is! The information I'm including is current material that will help authors connect with readers and produce their product in a professional manner. The copy that you are currently reading is now the 2016 Edition. As long as Amazon continues to abide by their current policies, readers will be alerted when newer editions become available, and they'll be able to download the updated book to their Kindles at no charge. And, if I want to change the title to show that it's the information available for the current year, I can do that too.

Play with the text, query your support group, and compare your titles and subtitles on your cover and product page to others in your genre. And, if you have a project similar to this book, you can always update the title to reflect the newer information. This is one of the advantages of self-publishing electronically. Confer with Amazon as you're making these changes. I can only share my experiences with you, and as mentioned they allowed me to update my content and add *2014, 2015,* and then *2016 Edition* to the title.

2. Synopsis

Your synopsis, or blurb, is the description of your story, or in the case of a nonfiction book, it's what you're offering the reader in terms of knowledge. Either way, it's a promise to the reader of what you're going to deliver within the pages of your book. While you're writing your book, you should try experimenting with different synopses. I keep an ongoing Word document open during the writing process, and I record ideas that I'll eventually try to use as part of my synopsis. As I mentioned, my online writing expert friends told me that my initial synopsis, for my first book, was weak and uninteresting. So I researched the correct ways to write a synopsis. I learned that it should be written in the present tense, no matter how your story is actually told. I learned that the point of view should be third person, because you want to give an immediate feel to the story, as though you're sitting across from your reader, sharing it directly with her or him. And, finally, I learned that I'm not very good at writing a synopsis. In fact, I'm very, very bad at it.

The second synopsis I used was written by a writer colleague from my support group, and he did a great job. I took his draft, altered it slightly, and used it when I did my initial upload. Bear in mind that you'll need different synopses of varying lengths for different purposes. You'll need a synopsis not only when you initially publish, but also when you're entering your work in different areas on Amazon's sites (utilizing Amazon's tools) and for different promotional opportunities that you participate in. Make sure you have a synopsis that's one hundred words, two hundred words, and one that's three hundred words too.

Since my first very poor attempt at writing a blurb or synopsis of my work, I've studied the blurbs of other books that are selling well. Some begin with a question. This attracts the reader's attention. Most have short, punchy sentences that make the reader take notice. And all of them describe the main plot and main characters. This is the method I use today when writing my synopsis. I play around with phrases and descriptions while I'm writing my book, and then I utilize some of the phrases from the comments that my beta readers give me in their analysis. Then I write several different synopses once I'm almost ready to upload. And at the end, I compare my finished blurb to the top books on Amazon and get it approved by the author colleagues in my support group. It's not necessary to describe your whole book (and also detrimental to do so) within your description. There's no magic to writing a good blurb. It has to attract readers, hold their attention, and make them want to know more. You make a promise, hint at what's to come, and do it in an engaging style.

You will change your blurb from time to time. I've altered or completely changed the description of my first book several times. I find inspiration for new blurbs in the reviews that readers write. Again, I keep an ongoing Word document and when I find a phrase that describes my story I save it, and if it works within a blurb I use it. This is one of the areas that you can use to freshen up your product presentation and possibly stimulate sales. Don't waste this opportunity. Continue to look for ideas. Our readers will see our story from a direction that we may not have, and their phraseology may be exactly what we need to write an enticing blurb. Use the tools that are at your disposal.

3. Formatting

Formatting isn't editing. Formatting is the process of readying your final product so that it can be downloaded into the system, which will thereby distribute your work in a format readable for said system. I know it sounds complicated but it isn't, because, if you're like me, you'll pay someone to do it.

When I first published my work, I wanted to reach as many readers as possible. Amazon has an exclusive program that you can enroll in; we mentioned it earlier. KDP Select requires you to have your work available only on Amazon's website, and they'll distribute your book to users who read books on Kindle reading devices. Or you can distribute your work through Amazon without enrolling in KDP Select. Additionally, Apple, Barnes & Noble, Kobo, and other stores sell e-books also. So I thought the best route for me was to distribute through every outlet in order to reach as many readers as I could. I live in Canada and unfortunately, as a Canadian resident, I can't upload directly to all of those outlets, so I released my book through Smashwords. Smashwords has a universal type of uploading process whereby they'll modify your manuscript and submit it to all of the above sites. They will also submit to Amazon, although this process is a little more complicated. They require you to sell over $2,000 worth of product through Smashwords, and then they will consider your submission to Amazon's catalog. In order to upload your work to Smashwords they offer a user's guide to help you do the modification, and there are numerous online resources that will help you with this. Or, as I said, you can pay someone to do it. That's what I did.

I want my work to stand spine-to-spine with any traditionally published book, and I want it to be every bit as professional, but my talents don't lie in the technical aspects of formatting from a Microsoft Word document to an epub or other type of document. I just want it to be done. So, unfortunately, this is one more place where, unless you're technically proficient enough to format your own work, you have to pay someone else to do it. I've listed the contact info for my formatter, Rich Meyer, in the *Helpful Links* section. Rich formatted the book you're currently reading.

Depending on the layout of your work and its length, formatting prices are usually under $100 for an average 70,000 word novel. If you include images and graphics the price will be higher.

The other advantage to paying to have your work formatted is that you have one more set of eyes going over your book, and you never know what your formatter might spot. Additionally, there are two other things you should make sure your formatter includes in your book.

A few months after my book was published Amazon contacted me and suggested that I include a table of contents. I'm not sure why a table of contents is important for a work of fiction, especially since the chapters aren't named and are only numbered, but I complied and had my formatter add a table of contents. I advise that when you format or have your work formatted, you include a linkable table of contents at the front of the book so readers can click on the chapter they want to access and have it show up on their Kindles.

Even more important than a table of contents is the inclusion of your contact information and links to your other works at the end of each book. Make sure that once the reader has finished reading your book, they have a way to contact you through email, your website, Facebook, and Twitter, if you have a Twitter presence also. Plus, if you have other books available, you should list the links to those at the end of your book too. Your formatter will ensure this is done correctly. In Chapter Eleven we talk about developing a media kit. This is one of the most useful tools you'll put together. I include a partial media kit at the end of my books. It includes direct links to all of my other work as well as access to my Facebook and Twitter feeds, plus my email address and website information.

A good formatter will also suggest that your acknowledgments appear at the end of the book or at least limit the acknowledgments that are up front. Amazon has a feature that allows readers to look inside the first few pages of your book before purchasing it. This way the potential purchasers can decide if the book is right for them. You definitely want to make sure you enable this feature when you download your book. This is the "Look Inside" option.

When readers check out the first few pages of your book, they don't want to read a lengthy list of acknowledgments. My suggestion is to list a simple, short acknowledgment near the beginning, and if you need a longer list of people who have helped and inspired you, put it at the end. This way your potential new readers can get a quick idea of your writing and decide whether they are going to take a chance on your book. If you have a long, drawn-out acknowledgment, there's always the possibility that they will click the little "x" and move on to the next book. For some time we've been recommending that you position your table of contents at the end of the book. Recently Amazon amended its publishing guidelines and now asks that we place the TOC at the beginning of the book. Kindle e-reader devices allow the reader to search out specific sections, so a table of contents, especially up front, really isn't necessary. In Chapter Eleven I've included updated information on the length and style of the back matter of your book.

If you'd still like to do your own formatting you can now upload your Word document directly to KDP's system. Or, if you'd like some help here's a free site that may help you: **calibre-ebook.com/**

CHAPTER FOUR HOMEWORK

1. Create a marketable title. Make sure it isn't being used by another bestselling book and query your support group in terms of its marketability.
2. Decide on subtitles for your book cover and product page. And, if possible, decide whether your book is going to be part of a series.
3. Write synopses of varying lengths. Compare them to blurbs of other bestselling books in your chosen category and query your support system. Utilize help wherever you can find it. Use phrases or content that comes from your betas, colleagues, or anybody who can give you a catchy, fresh way to describe your book.
4. Find a formatter or format your own work. Formatters are available through your support group or by asking in forums. If one name keeps coming up and the price quotes you receive are reasonable, then you've probably found your new formatter. Or if you decide to format yourself don't worry; Amazon has a tool that will allow you to examine your work before it goes live on their site.

CHAPTER THREE FOLLOW-UP

1. Now that you've had your cover for a little while, do you still like it? A good cover should grow on you, and you should like it the longer you have it. Once you've sold a gazillion thousand copies it might become old, but at this point you should still be proud of your cover. If you're not, go back to the points in Chapter Three

and start over again and find yourself a new cover. I've said it before and I'll say it again: a cover is extremely important.

2. Are you continuing to network and "pay it forward"? As you learn information are you sharing it with other authors? The dividends from this will become clearer as we go along. The self-publishing community has been built on one author helping another and it's important that we continue to do this.

CHAPTER FIVE
CHOOSING A PLATFORM
Or
How I Pissed Off Smashwords, Sony, and Apple

We all have a story to tell, don't we? And, as you've probably determined by this point, my self-publishing journey is full of stories. Let me tell you one, and I tell you this in the hope that it will help you decide where you want to sell your book. As I mentioned previously, when my work was ready to publish, I had some choices to make.

It's estimated that Amazon currently sells 65% of all e-books sold. There are other outlets too, though. There's Apple, Kobo, and Barnes & Noble, just to name a few. At the time of my initial publishing attempt, as an author residing in Canada, most of the non-Amazon outlets wouldn't allow me to publish directly to their sites. That was disappointing because there are a lot of Kobo e-readers sold in Canada. In fact, in Canada, the Kindle device, Amazon's e-reader, is neck and neck with the Kobo in sales. Kobo is also the e-reader of choice that Chapters, our main bookseller, sells. Plus I had friends who owned Kobo readers, and I wanted them to be able to read my book, too. So, in order to accommodate everybody, and to see my work on Chapter's website, I published through Smashwords, which in turn distributed my work through their affiliates (Kobo, Apple, Barnes & Noble, and all the others).

Smashwords is a company founded by Mark Coker. Mark is a well-known figure in the self-publishing community, and he's done more for self-published authors than almost anyone else. His company has helped get a lot of books into general circulation that otherwise would not have found readers. Smashwords will distribute your e-book to all of the major online stores including Barnes & Noble, Apple, Kobo, and (if your Smashwords sales exceed $2,000), Amazon. So I published my book through Smashwords but uploaded directly to Amazon separately. I hired a formatter, and he formatted an e-book for Smashwords and one for Amazon.

I was now a published author with my book available on multiple websites. This, again, was the point where I was sitting back, waiting for the world to acknowledge my brilliance and send the accolades my way. And, as you know by now, it didn't happen. In two months, after trying numerous sales and marketing strategies, I sold about two hundred e-books. The vast majority of those sales were through Amazon's site. Even though I wanted to sell lots of books in my own country, the largest market is the United States. That's where most of the readers are and that's where Amazon lives.

As I read blogs and discovered how many e-books were being sold by other Indie authors, I wondered what I was doing wrong. I tried $0.99 sales, I ran ads on Facebook and Goodreads, and I held a Facebook event. None of these ventures helped me reach the number of readers that the top bestselling Indie authors were reaching.

One of the frustrations I was having was that the reviews coming in confirmed what my beta readers had told me earlier: I had a pretty good book. All of the reviews at that point were five-star reviews. I had readers from all over the world telling me how much they enjoyed *My Temporary Life*. Some even called it the best book they had read in years, but I just couldn't reach that next level of sales.

I thought it might help if I had more reviews, and this was a good tactic. I personally always check out the reviews of books, movies, hotels, or resorts before I pick one. So I submitted my book to countless review sites. I'll detail this process more thoroughly later on, as it's an extremely important part of your overall strategy. The reviewers who were kind enough to review my book all came back with positive comments. I was fortunate enough to still be receiving five stars from everywhere.

As I lurked around Kboards, Amazon Author Discussions, KDP Community Forums, and the Facebook writers groups that I belonged to, one topic was discussed over and over: KDP Select. None of the authors in my support group had enrolled in KDP Select, so I didn't know much about it. I was about to receive an email that would change everything.

As your book gets read and enjoyed, you'll receive emails and messages from readers. This is one of the best parts of writing. I had put together a website by that point and had my website address and email contact listed at the back of my book, plus I was all over Facebook, Twitter, and Amazon's Author Central (to be discussed as part of utilizing Amazon's tools in Chapter Seven). I was easily accessible and received some very nice emails and messages from readers who had enjoyed my book. One of the emails was from a gentleman who was in the process of coercing his wife into reading *My Temporary Life*. He had enjoyed my book so much that he told me he'd given her a choice. Either she read the book or she had to pack her bags. Thankfully she read the book and enjoyed it.

I started a correspondence with this gentleman and really enjoyed our exchanges. One important question to ask readers is how they found you. Once your book is live, you're going to find that the main question you have is "Where are the readers?" I always try to ask people who've read my work how they heard about it. Were they browsing Amazon's site, did they read an interview I'd done, or was it a referral? This particular gentleman had been referred to my work by another Indie author.

I contacted the author who had referred my work and discovered that he had published his book a few months before mine, but he'd found a lot more readers than I had. I researched his book to see if I could figure out what he was doing differently from me, and I emailed him thanking him for the referral. This started a dialogue and exchange of ideas. As we traded strategies, I learned that his book had hit the top ten overall rankings on Amazon. This is an incredibly significant achievement, and not a lot of self-published books had gotten there at that time. After a while, the author shared his secret with me. He'd enrolled in Amazon's KDP Select program, and he encouraged me to do the same. Actually, his words were, "Don't forget me when you're rich and famous."

Even though conversations between authors regarding KDP Select were more in favor of being non-exclusive and distributing your work everywhere as opposed to being exclusively with KDP Select, there was something about the way he said it that excited me, and I couldn't wait to enroll. That's when I ran into some roadblocks.

KDP Select, as I mentioned, is an Amazon program. As an author you can enroll in KDP Select for ninety days, but you have to offer your work exclusively through them. You can't be published anywhere else. The benefits today are that you can utilize Amazon's free promotional tool and give away your book, run a Kindle Countdown Deal promotion, be paid for borrows from the Kindle Owners' Lending Library, and receive royalties from the Kindle Unlimited program. At that point, at the beginning of 2012, authors were finding it extremely beneficial to give away their books. The way the system works is that during the ninety-day enrollment period, you can offer your book for free for up to a maximum of five days. We're going to examine free promotions in detail later in Chapter Nine, and this tactic is not as foolproof as it once was. At that point though, it was an almost sure-fire method of selling books. There was, and still is, a process that must be followed, but at the end of 2011 and beginning of 2012, authors were having success. They were giving away their books and then often enjoying a huge surge in paid sales once their books returned to the retail price.

The additional benefit to having your book enrolled in KDP Select, as mentioned, is the revenue you'll be paid from borrows and page reads. There are two separate programs that you'll be able to take advantage of. Amazon Prime is a program that Amazon customers in several countries can enroll in. They pay an annual fee, and this entitles customers to discounted or sometimes even free shipping, access to the Amazon video library, plus access to the Kindle Owners' Lending Library. By being a member of this library, you can borrow one book a month. So, as an author, when you have your book enrolled in KDPS, you're paid for these borrows. Additionally, the Kindle Unlimited program pays you per page read every time a customer who has enrolled in KU reads part of your book. Kindle Unlimited is a Netflix-type offering where a customer can access thousands of books for a monthly fee. Both of these are terrific sources of additional revenue for authors enrolled in KDP Select. In Chapter Nine I'll show you how to maximize the amount of borrows and page reads you can earn from both of these programs.

The more I researched Select and heard success stories from other authors the more I wanted to participate. I couldn't wait to unpublish my book from Smashwords (and its affiliates), and enroll exclusively with KDPS. Unfortunately, this wasn't the easiest thing in the world to do.

I went through the process on the Smashwords site and unpublished my work, and I received an email from a representative telling me that my book would be completely removed from all of their affiliates' sites in four to six weeks. Amazon wanted exclusivity and I was ready to give it to them, but I didn't want to wait for Smashwords to set me free. I read blogs and forum threads detailing the steps other authors had gone through trying to have their work removed from some of the affiliates' sites. The stories weren't good. All of them had waited weeks to have their books free and clear. Some authors cheated and enrolled in KDPS while their books were still for sale elsewhere. They'd been found out of course, and Amazon removed their books altogether.

I didn't want to wait weeks before joining KDPS, so I emailed each of the affiliate stores individually. This included Sony (who are no longer in the e-book business), Apple, Barnes & Noble, and Diesel. I told each of them I had informed Smashwords that my book was no longer available to them and they did not have permission to sell it, and I asked them to please remove it right away. Within twenty-four hours I had emails from all of them. Sony even asked me to email them my phone number so they could call me. And then, Mark Coker emailed me too. He'd received an email from Apple's legal department (which was where my email to them ended up). Mark wanted to know what was going on. At that time I wasn't the only author leaving Smashwords to join KDPS; there were others too, and I suspect Mark probably knew that. I kindly asked him to remove my book.

Twenty-four hours later, my book was unpublished and not available anywhere. Sony, in their phone call to me, even apologized about the delay. In hindsight, it was a good move for me to enroll in KDPS when I did, and I'll explain in Chapter Nine why my timing was very, very fortunate, but it was unfortunate that I had to do it the way that I did. As I mentioned, Smashwords, Mr. Coker, and everyone at their affiliates were extremely nice to me; I just didn't want to have to wait. And possibly at some point, if they'll have me, I'll publish through Smashwords again. At the time though, it was important to leave their system as quickly as I could.

My journey into KDP Select was due to another author's referral, but it was more than that. I got lucky, and as you'll see in the coming chapters, my timing was extremely fortunate, but it was also because I was listening and asking questions. I queried my support group and other authors who were succeeding, and I tried to surround myself with successful people. This goes back to what we talked about at the beginning of this process. Network, follow blogs, listen to what's happening in the self-publishing community, and most of all have a support group that will tell you the truth. How I rose and fell and rose again with KDPS is detailed later, but none of it would have happened if it weren't for the relationships I cultivated and nurtured with folks who knew far more than I did, and that's what we're going to look at next.

CHAPTER FIVE HOMEWORK

1. Pick a distribution outlet. Look at Smashwords' site and Amazon's site. Take a look at Barnes & Noble, and Apple's sites where they sell e-books. Check out the recent discussions on forums and groups and query your support group. What's working and where are books being sold most effectively?
2. Continue to participate in groups and forums in a respectful manner. Keep your eye on which promotional opportunities are working for other authors.
3. Promote the work of those you believe in. Your support group should include authors whose work you admire; promote them on your Facebook page.

CHAPTER FOUR FOLLOW-UP

1. How's your synopsis? It'll never be in its final form because you'll alter and modify it even after you've published, but are you happy

with it? Do you have different versions in varying lengths?

2. Is your work completely formatted? Is it ready to be uploaded? You should have received it back from your formatter by now. Get ready; it's almost time to upload your book into the system.

CHAPTER SIX
RELATIONSHIPS AND PRE-LAUNCH STRATEGIES
Or
I'll Like Yours If You Like Mine

This is a good time for us to take a break from the technical tasks we've been working on and deal with something a little more personal. Throughout this book I've talked about relationships. I've talked about paying it forward: trying to help others succeed and how this ultimately helps us too. And I've talked about the target that we self-published authors have on our backs. Unfortunately, when an Indie author publishes a book that uses previously released material (plagiarism), or an author pays for reviews (unethical), or an author's formatting is out of sync (amateurish), apart from just simply being wrong, this reflects on all of us. Remember, we're being examined so closely because of the degree of success e-books and Indie authors have achieved in such a short period of time. If we weren't selling books and connecting with readers, nobody would be paying any attention to us.

Earlier, when we talked about picking our support team, I mentioned how some authors try to game the system and approach self-publishing in a less scrupulous manner. There will always be these types of individuals, and we all have our own lines in the sand, or things we will and won't do. As you continue along your path you'll learn how to determine those who are operating their business with integrity and those who aren't. You will learn who's really selling books and who isn't, too, and of course you want to surround yourself with successful writers who are selling books and connecting with readers. One of the ways you can tell how many books an author is selling is by referring to Theresa Ragan's chart. Theresa is a successful Indie author and again, like the others we've mentioned, she's a big supporter of other Indies. She's been kind enough to share her chart here: **www.theresaragan.com/salesrankingchart.html.**

As you can see, it's very easy to tell from a book's ranking approximately how many books are being sold. When I run a promotion on *My Temporary Life*, or even on one of my other books, *My Temporary Life* runs up the rankings and I sell a number of books. When I'm not running a promotion (which probably means I'm working on a new book), it's usually in the 40,000 to 80,000 range in overall ranking. According to Theresa's chart, that puts me in the 1 to 5 books per day range, and that is indeed accurate.

In addition to being aware of whom you're forming contacts with, it's important to cultivate and build relationships with the folks who can help you too. And, while we're looking at relationships, we're going to begin preparation for your book launch, because both things are connected, and because we're almost there.

1. Website Administrators
2. "Like-Fests" and Facebook Groups
3. Beta Readers and Reviewers

1. Website Administrators

When I have the opportunity to speak to writing groups and conferences, one of the things I like to talk about is that promotional opportunities sometimes come to me these days. Fortunately, I don't have to hunt them down the way I did when I first published. Bear in mind I'm not a veteran self-publisher or author. My first book went live in December 2011. As you read this book, I'll have six titles published, and I hope to have one more released by the end of 2016. I don't know everything; I'm still learning, just like you are. There are certainly authors reaching more readers than I and authors consistently earning more than I do, but I've developed a way of working that I'm very happy with.

When I ran my first free promotion for *My Temporary Life*, two major websites featured free books. It was imperative to be promoted on both of those sites in order to have an effective free run. I was very fortunate. Both **www.pixelofink.com** and **www.ereadernewstoday.com** promoted my book. Today, both are still relevant, but there are others too. Don't worry; we're going to talk specifically about all of them when we develop a marketing plan for your book in Chapters Nine and Ten.

When those two sites featured me, I went from having a moderately successful promotion to hitting it out of the park. So, when the dust settled, I went back and emailed everyone who helped promote my book, including the two major sites, and thanked them.

There are two sites that will monitor where you or your book is being talked about: Google Alerts **www.google.com/alerts** and Mention **https://en.mention.net/**. Both of these programs are free (although Mention does have a paid option, which I've never felt the need to sign up for). You type in your search word or phrase and they'll troll the Internet looking for your book title, author name, or whatever else you're trying to find, and they'll email you an alert when they find it. I prefer Mention.net, as it seems to have more acute search capabilities than Google. By using these two programs you'll be up to date on who's helping get the word out about your book. And you'll be able to contact each source afterward and thank them. Plus if a pirate site is selling your book illegally it'll seek that out too. We'll discuss piracy sites when we talk about the Business of Writing in Chapter Eleven.

I take this one step further. When I began building a presence on Facebook groups and different forums, I started receiving invites to write blogs for other writers websites and other Indie writing sites. Don't worry; these opportunities will come, and you should always take advantage of them. Not only are they a great way to reach more readers, it's also a way to pay back the sites that helped you. When I write blogs, if there's a site that has featured me, I try to mention them, and their site address, of course. Then I email the website and include the link to the blog where I mentioned them. This is just smart online networking and a great way of paying back. Over time it's helped me build relationships with some of the folks who run the sites that promote Indie books.

From those relationships and friendships that you develop, you may receive opportunities that other authors may not get. For example, sometimes an author will back out of an ad. If you have a relationship with the owner of the site, the opportunity to substitute your book may come your way. I'm often alerted when new promotional features are offered. I'm not special; I've just built the relationships and given credit where credit was due in terms of spreading the word about a promotion that has worked well for me.

2. "Like-Fests" and Facebook Groups

I extend the same courtesy in the Facebook groups and forums I frequent. During any type of promotion I always politely ask for assistance, and then afterward I revisit the site or group and thank them for their help. This is not a "like-fest" that I'm referring to. This is just common courtesy that helps build the relationships with the folks who are in a position to get the word out about your book.

What's that question you're asking? Yes, I can hear you now. What's a "like-fest"? On your Facebook page, occasionally on your book's product page (although Amazon has now removed this feature), and in other areas where you will be promoting your work, there is often a "like" button. This gives the reader the opportunity to click the button and acknowledge that they agree with your post or like your work. At one time, the more "likes" you received, the more prominently your post was displayed. With some exceptions (Facebook), "likes" don't fuel your passage to popularity the way they did at one point but they are still important.

Sometimes a group will orchestrate a managed "like-fest." This is where you "like" someone else's site, book, or posting, and they'll return the favor. Lots of groups do it. In fact, there are Facebook groups that have been specifically created to only do this.

This is a good idea but, and this is where my personal line in the sand appears, I'll only "like" a post or book if I do indeed actually like it. Confused? I hope not. Amazon began enforcing its review policies more vigorously toward the end of 2012. A number of authors, some traditionally published and some self-published, were caught posting false, or forged, reviews. Names were named, apologies (and unfortunately excuses too) were made, and Amazon tightened up its review system. So now, if a review appears to be written by someone at the same computer (or IP) address as the writer of the book, or if the review seems suspicious, Amazon will remove it. This is a good thing. Anything that keeps the system honest and improves credibility is good. When this happened, it forced me to look at "likes," and I decided I'd only endorse a book if I believed in it. From time to time I'll promote a book on my Facebook page or on Twitter, and if I do, I've either read the book or I know enough about it to believe in it. Where you draw your line is up to you, but remember that this is a transparent industry and everybody is watching, so my suggestion would be that if you're going to support someone's work be sure you do indeed believe in it.

3. Beta Readers and Reviewers

Now that I've given you my holier-than-thou speech, let's talk about reviewers and beta readers once again. When I published my first book, I knew I needed reviews. Some were coming in, but I felt that if I could find a way to get more reviews for my book, word of mouth would catch fire and I'd reach more readers, so I found a way. Amazon has lists of its top reviewers. These are folks whose reviews are read and respected by lots of readers— yes, the readers who purchase books just like yours and mine. I found the list and filtered it down until I had the reviewers who enjoyed reading fiction and read e-books, and then I emailed them. I emailed almost one hundred of them. The link is in the *Helpful Links* sheet, but for your quick reference, here it is:

www.amazon.com/review/top-reviewers.

As you can see, some of them have their contact info listed, and some even have their own websites. From the requests I sent out, I received reviews from a number of very well respected reviewers. Once I went through the learning curve of realizing that you have to check each of their websites to learn exactly how to submit, things went a lot smoother. Thankfully, I had a couple of kind reviewers walk me through the protocol involved in submitting to review sites. This is where relationship building is especially important. If you find reviewers who enjoy reading your work, they'll want to read your next book, and of course, they'll get the word out to their followers too.

Some of the top review sites are run by bloggers and reviewers with followers in the hundreds and sometimes even thousands. From a single review, you can reach a lot of potential readers. Plus, these reviewers read a lot, and it's important to get honest feedback from an expert in order for us to progress as writers. Again, if those multimillion bestselling authors are trying to become better writers, we better make sure we're doing the same.

In addition to canvassing Amazon's reviewers, there are a number of review sites that you can submit your book to. I've included a list of current sites in the *Helpful Links* sheet at the back of the book. Remember to examine the submission requirements before submitting. Just like the Amazon reviewers, each site or blogger has a specific set of parameters, and it's to no one's advantage if you submit your gothic horror novel to a reviewer who's seeking contemporary romance. And, bear in mind, some reviewers do not review self-published work. Yes, I know, we will change this attitude, but it's going to take some time.

It's also important to remember not to blindly copy and paste the same email to multiple sites; you need to read their requirements. I suggest you check out their most recent posted reviews. Unfortunately you will find that some reviewers, although their criteria states they'll accept self-published books, still hold us under the microscope a little more intently than they might a traditionally published book. There are prejudices that haven't yet gone away. Examine the type of books the reviewer has read, and make sure their analysis is delivered in a constructive fashion. Make your choices wisely before submitting your work.

Even though the lists in the *Helpful Links* section shows lengthy lists of reviewers, many of them are severely backed up in terms of workload. That's why it's important to submit, submit, submit, and submit now. Yes, right now, even though you haven't published yet. In a couple of chapters' time, we're going to talk about your book launch, and one of the most important factors—getting reviews quickly. Even though your book is still unpublished, vet out the reviewers you feel will want to read your work, make sure you follow their submission requirements, and get ready to send out lots of books.

The format in which you send your books will vary. Some reviewers and bloggers will accept a PDF copy of your work while others want an actual gifted copy from Amazon. For them you'll have to wait until you've uploaded your work into the system. Or, you can email your Word file directly to their Kindle device. Send your file as an attachment to this address in order to place it directly on their reading device.

Some websites will ask you to pay in order to see a more extensive or updated list of reviewer sites. Don't pay the fee. And certainly don't pay a reviewer to review your book. If you'd like more review sites than the ones I've included, query your support team or ask on Kboards or KDP Community Forums. It's your business to know these things, and as you interact with other authors, you'll find this information is easy to come by.

The other source for reviews is, of course, the beta readers who so kindly read your book toward the beginning of this process. Usually they're very willing to post a review for you. Your beta readers are professional readers. I've developed friendships with many of my beta readers while some have elected to keep the relationship professional and interact only when I have a book to submit for their opinion. The reviews you'll receive from your beta readers will vary, just as they will from any reader. You can't and shouldn't expect only positive reviews from them. Even though they've helped in the development of your work, they're going to compare it to other books they've read. Their opinions, just like any other readers who've read your book, are their own opinions. If they've put in the time, and in the case of folks who've purchased your work, their money too, they can write what they want.

Also, bear in mind that although we're primarily talking about posting reviews on Amazon, there are other sites where reviews are important. The prominent readers' site where reviews are crucial is Goodreads, and we'll talk about Goodreads in the next chapter. So, when courteously asking your beta readers to review your book and submitting to reviewers, ask them to post a review on Goodreads as well as Amazon and any other reader sites they may frequent.

From time to time you'll be presented with other opportunities from reviewers. Some will be legitimate and some won't be. Shortly after I released my first book, I received an email from a reviewer in the southern United States. She claimed to write for a number of newspapers and asked if I could send her a print copy of my book, as she didn't read on an e-reader. I took a chance and mailed her a copy of my book and fortunately, she enjoyed it very much. Subsequently I was featured in a number of newspapers in the Alabama area, and when my second book came out, the reviewer was kind enough to feature it also. That lady has become a great supporter of my work, and every time I receive an email from a reader in the Alabama area I know exactly whom to thank. So you never know. Follow your instinct and continue to build relationships with reviewers and your beta readers. Here's an article I wrote on correct protocol when dealing with reviewers:

www.indiesunlimited.com/2013/07/02/for-the-love-of-the-book/

As you've probably just determined, the secret to having promotional opportunities come to you is quite simple. You build and nurture relationships with other authors, bloggers, reviewers, website administrators, and your beta readers, and pay back when you can. You're going to be invited to write blogs for your colleagues' websites as well as other Indie author sites. These opportunities will come as you build a presence on forums and groups and as your books begin to sell too. Always take these opportunities. It'll definitely help you broaden your scope and find more readers, and also give you the ability to pay it back to the folks who have helped you, whether it's another author or an influential site that has featured you..

One of the great thrills I experienced a few months after I published was being asked to contribute a monthly article to Indies Unlimited. I've referred you to many of their articles throughout this book, so you probably realize by now that the mandate at IU is to help other authors. They do this on a volunteer basis, and it was exactly the type of environment I wanted to be a part of. Because of the articles I've written for them, I've had invites galore. I've now had the pleasure of writing for a number of different sites. Some I'd never heard of and some I had. It's been a great experience. I've listed below the basic rules or philosophy I employ when building relationships. In other words, this is my own personal line in the sand.

1. Share everything. If you've found a site that is effective in promoting your book, share it. Or, if you've found a reviewer who's looking for new material, share the reviewer's information. Your colleagues are going to find it sooner or later anyway, so why not earn yourself a reputation as someone who gives and spreads that positive energy around.

2. Ask nicely, thank, and then give credit where credit is due. Make sure you respect the rules of the groups and forums you participate in, and if you're given some assistance, take the time to go back and thank the group and the folks who helped you. Remember, they're not just smiley little icons or these things @ with their names after them. They're real people.

3. Treat reviewers with respect and try to build relationships with them. You're going to interact with reviewers each time you release a book. And you never know, the reviewer who has one hundred followers today might have twenty thousand by the time you release your next book. It happens all the time!

4. Accept the criticism. I want to become a better writer, and I'm going to accomplish this by practicing writing and listening to my readers and reviewers. If someone has put in the time to read your work, and especially if they paid money for it, then they're entitled to post a review with their thoughts.

CHAPTER SIX HOMEWORK

1. Determine what your personal philosophy is going to be; find your line in the sand. Decide whether you're comfortable "liking" work in order to support other writers, or if you feel you need to be more familiar with their books before endorsing them to your followers.

2. Sign up for Google Alerts and Mention. These sites will help you keep track of where you're being talked about and by whom.

3. Save Theresa Ragan's rankings chart, and if you find it useful, drop her an email and thank her. She'd love to hear from you.

4. Submit your work to review sites. Find reviewers through Amazon's top reviewer list and through the lists I've provided, and submit your work to them. Indicate that you haven't published yet but are looking for reviews in order to have a successful book launch. Submit to as many sites as you have the energy to work at. These are busy folks, and not all of them will be able to read your work.

5. Request reviews from your beta readers, and remember, ask everybody to post not only on Amazon but Goodreads and any other reader sites they frequent.

CHAPTER FIVE FOLLOW-UP

1. Which platform have you decided on? Smashwords? Amazon? KDP Select? You can change afterward, but your initial launch is critical, so make sure you've made the correct choice.

2. Are you querying your colleagues and answering their questions where you can? If the relationships you currently have aren't working, you may need to find different members for your support group. Don't hesitate to bring new writers into your own personal circle.

3. Are your Facebook page and Twitter feed diverse enough or are they becoming one long commercial? Make sure you're mixing it up and not only concentrating on promoting yourself and others.

CHAPTER SEVEN
UTILIZING AMAZON'S TOOLS
Or
Google Doesn't Know Everything

I had lots of help publishing and marketing my novels. That's one of the advantages of the pay it forward community that we're a part of, and yes, if you've read this far, you're a part of it too. As I mentioned earlier, when I was stuck with minimal sales and couldn't find a way to expand my readership, I contacted Robert Bidinotto. Robert gave me a number of different suggestions, and one of the things he said was that I should "utilize Amazon's tools." So, after I changed my cover and rewrote my synopsis, I decided to tackle this next part of the process. The only problem was that I didn't know what he meant. I didn't know what Amazon's tools were. I searched their website, and the only tools it showed were hammers and screwdrivers for sale in their online store. I didn't need those types of tools.

So I went to the real online encyclopedia of knowledge. I Googled "Amazon's Tools." That still didn't help. All that came back were links to forums where other authors were asking, "What are Amazon's tools?" Obviously I wasn't the only one Robert had helped. Google didn't have an answer. So between the other members of my support group and myself (because at that point Robert had been far too kind with his time and I didn't want to impose on him further), we discovered what they are, and I'm going to share that knowledge with you. You'll take advantage of some of these tools after you've hit the upload button and some beforehand. I'm going to include them all here because it's simpler to deal with them as one large unit.

1. **Categories and Genres**
2. **Keywords and Tags**
3. **Pricing**
4. **Product Page**
5. **Goodreads**
6. **Author Central**
7. **Amazon Affiliate Program**
8. **CreateSpace**

1.   Categories and Genres

We've talked about your chosen genre and categories throughout this book, and hopefully your book falls clearly into a recognized genre. If you're writing a romance or thriller novel, you're in luck, as those categories are extremely popular. If that's not the case and your genre falls under the "unclassifiable" label, I can still help you, because that's where my books seem to end up.

Up until my last book, I had trouble writing a traditional, easily recognizable, falls within the lines kind of story to save myself. My first book has been classified as literary fiction, romance, suspense, thriller, and coming of age. And, unfortunately, all of those labels are accurate. This is a good and bad thing. It's good in that it gives me some options, but it's bad in that it's not a traditional genre novel that falls within the acceptable boundaries. When it comes to marketing, that can make it more difficult to discover where my readers are. But, when it came to picking categories, it did give me some options.

You're going to have the opportunity to pick categories in several areas. When you first upload your e-book you'll be able to choose two categories. And if you're producing a print book through Amazon's print-on-demand company, CreateSpace, you'll be permitted to pick categories there too. The most important ones are first though. You need to decide which two categories you're going to pick for your e-book when you enter your information to KDP (Amazon).

This is an exciting time because two steps from now, you're going to upload your book and become a published author, but don't rush this part of the process; categories are very important. Some categories on Amazon are extremely crowded and populated not just by a lot of books but also by a lot of good books too, some written by bestselling authors. When I first uploaded my book, I jumped right into the fray and picked Romantic/Suspense as my category, and although I switch from time to time as I seek out readers who may be searching in different areas, I tend to keep coming back to Romantic/Suspense.

It's a hot category; my novel fits into it, and a lot of readers are looking for that type of book. When *My Temporary Life* peaked in February 2012, it hit #1 in Romantic/Suspense and stayed there for almost two weeks. It was a magical time. I jumped over established authors and I was outselling them every day. Unfortunately it didn't last, but I was in the game, trying and winning, or at least for a little while. So, as of this writing, I'm currently still categorized under Romantic/Suspense, and when *My Temporary Life* peaks, as it does from time to time, I'm in a category where there are lots of readers looking for books.

I've played around with several different categories as my second choice. Your second category should be in a genre that is more winnable. It should be less populated and more specific than your first choice, while still being relevant to your plot. Currently, when you look at my book's product page on Amazon, my second category, the consistently winnable one, looks like this: <u>Kindle Store</u> > <u>Kindle eBooks</u> > <u>Literature & Fiction</u> > <u>Drama</u> > **British & Irish**

These are the popularity charts, and they're the most important rankings on Amazon because that's where readers are diverted to when they're browsing for books. I'm consistently in the top thirty of the category noted above, and from time to time, as my sales rise, I hit the #1 position. When you're in the #1 position, Amazon places a badge beside your book, on the search pages, indicating that your book is a #1 bestseller in that category. This gives readers one more reason to possibly check out your book. It's very important that I get to compete with the major writers in the Romantic/Suspense category, but I also want to show that my book is selling. So my book is in two categories that are still relevant, but one that is more popular and populous than the other.

When you're choosing your categories, it's best to once again visit Amazon's Kindle store and then scroll through the categories listed on the left-hand side of the page. You'll find this by going to **www.amazon.com** and clicking on the "Kindle e-books" tab near the top of the page. As you click on each one they'll become more specific. For example, I can click on "Kindle e-books," and make it more specific by clicking on "Literature and Fiction," and finally click on "Literary Fiction." Each category lists how many books are available. Assuming that there are over four million e-books for sale in the Kindle store (yep, there are), I go from that very large number to about one hundred and twenty-five thousand in "Literature and Fiction," and then I can pare it down even further to about twenty-five thousand in "Literary Fiction." By doing this I know how many books I'm competing against. And, if I go to the top books in that category, I'll see where their overall ranks are and that'll tell me (by using Theresa Ragan's rankings chart), approximately how many books they're selling daily. From there I can get a pretty good idea of how many books I need to sell to become a bestseller in that category.

The only challenge, with choosing a less-populated category is that when you choose categories, right before you're about to upload your work onto Amazon's site, all of the categories are not available in the drop-down menu. At the bottom of the drop-down there is a category labeled "non-classifiable." Click on this when you're choosing your second category. From there, go to the Contact section on the same page. From there, email Amazon, and ask to have your book included in the less-populated category. As long as your book does indeed belong there, they will include you.

Here's a short reminder list on how to pick your categories:

a) *On Amazon.com click the "Kindle Store" on the left side of the page. Amazon changes the terminology and position from time to time, so it may also be referred to as "Kindle e-books and readers."*

b) *Scroll down the left side of the page and continue clicking on categories until you find a fit for your book.*

c) *Pick a popular category that applies to your book that has a high number of books in the parentheses.*

d) *Pick a less popular category that applies to your book that has a low number of books in the parentheses.*

e) *Click on the less populous category and see what the overall ranking is for the number one book. If you feel the overall number is a ranking you can attain or beat then choose this category (if it's a fit for your book).*

f) *On your KDP dashboard under "Target Your Book To Customers" (currently used terminology) click on the drop-down menu and choose the popular, heavily populated category.*

g) *As your second choice, from your dashboard choose the bottom selection "Non-Classifiable."*

h) *At the bottom right side of the same page of your dashboard click on "Contact Us." In your message to Amazon let them know which category you'd like as your Non-Classifiable choice based on the choice you made in d).*

That, in a nutshell, is how to specifically develop a marketing plan that will enable you to get your book to bestseller status. Hopefully your book will reach #1 in the heavily populated category and you sell a whole bunch of books, but if you don't, or if you don't at first, then at least you've got a chance at bestseller status with this two-pronged approach. Jim Devitt wrote about it in an excellent article for, yep, them again, Indies Unlimited. Jim's article has gone on to become one of the most read posts in the history of their site. The Indies Unlimited folks have agreed to share it with you here: **www.indiesunlimited.com/2012/03/17/helping-you-become-a-1-bestselling-author/.**

2. Keywords and Tags

Once you pick and enter your categories, you'll be asked to choose keywords that describe your book. As we mentioned earlier, when a reader types a search term into Amazon's search bar, the system searches your title, subtitle, and the keywords you've entered. So, in addition to the titles and subtitles that we picked earlier, your keywords are an extremely important and often overlooked task. Your book is about to compete with a lot of other books on Amazon's site, and if you're like me, you'll want to go after the big guns. We need to be confident in our work. Up to this point, we've gone through all the proper processes and we believe in ourselves, so even though we're being practical, and approaching self-publishing as a business, we all have a dream. And we dream that our book is just as good as, or perhaps even better than, the bestselling books that we're going to compete against.

Once again, go to Amazon's Kindle site. Then, in the search bar, put in some keywords that are relevant to your book's description. If the books that come up are highly ranked and in your category, and again, are relevant to your book, you may want to consider using those words. It's an interesting process, and although I'd advise against spending hours trying to determine exactly the correct keywords, it's still important to find ones that are going to help readers find your book. All of the tools that we're currently utilizing are intended to help spread your virtual wings as wide as possible. If you had a print book and were able to place one book on as many shelves in the store as you could, you'd do it, and that's what we're doing now. We want your name, book title, cover, and synopsis to be everywhere that it can. If Amazon is giving us an opportunity to enter our information, we want to do that as often and as efficiently as possible.

For some reason we seem to have a tendency to want to be very specific with the keywords we use. This doesn't help us. We want the search term to be as broad as possible in order to reach as many readers as we can. Avoid using specific words. Concentrate on the popular and most recently used terms that apply to your book.

Bestselling Indie author Martin Hengst was kind enough to send me this very important information. This is taken directly from KDP's Help Section:

In order to list your title in certain sub-categories, you'll need to add Search Keywords in addition to the categories you choose for your title. Click a category in the list below to see the keyword requirements.

Biographies & Memoirs

Business & Money

Children's eBooks

Comics & Graphic Novels

Erotica

Health, Fitness, & Dieting

History

LGBT

Literature & Fiction

Mystery, Thriller, & Suspense

Religion & Spirituality

Romance

Science Fiction & Fantasy

Teen & Young Adult

Textbooks

Here's the link to this section:

**https://kdp.amazon.com/self-
publishing/help?topicId=A200PDGPEIQX41**

As you can see, some categories correspond with select keywords. So, if you're writing in one of the above categories, make sure you use the appropriate keywords. Failing to do this might result in Amazon listing your book in an inappropriate category. Since the original publication of this book, multiple new categories were added that require specific keywords. These categories are listed above for your convenience. Unfortunately this is not an area where the information is widely publicized, and not all authors are familiar with the "Categories with Keywords Requirements" section. If your book currently is not listed as one of the applicable categories, keep this information and the link handy. New categories are being added all the time. The above categories with keywords requirement section is for Amazon US only. When you click on the above link you'll see the requirements differ from country to country. It only takes a few minutes to make sure you're in compliance.

Tags are currently not being used by Amazon. Tags were search words that you could add at the bottom of your product page to help readers find your book. Hopefully they won't come back into usage, as they were being manipulated by some. For example, instead of typing in a search term as a tag, some less scrupulous or less informed authors would type in their own names, hoping to piggyback some success from the tagged book. If they do come back, I'm sure Amazon will have some stricter controls on them. If tags come back the same guidelines apply as above. Pick search terms that are popular and relevant to your work. Spread your wings as wide as possible and help readers find your book.

3. Pricing

Ah, the favorite topic: how much to charge. How much is too much and how much isn't enough? And how does that affect how you're paid, or does it affect how you're paid? Well, it does affect how you're paid, and how much to charge is up to you. You're the boss. The price of your book should be whatever the market will bear. In other words, you need to find your sweet spot and stay there.

Amazon will pay you a 70% royalty on the price of your e-book if your pricing is between $2.99 and $9.99. If your price is below or above those numbers, they'll pay you 35%. You'll change your price during certain promotions, and we're going to outline that in Chapter Nine. Occasionally, you'll drop below $2.99 for a limited time, but don't go above $9.99. I was disappointed recently when two of my favorite traditionally published authors released new books and their e-books were priced higher than their print books. As a reader, that doesn't work for me. I don't mind paying a premium price for an e-book from an established author whose work I know I'm going to enjoy, but knowing what I know about publishing, there's no reason that prices should be so high. That brings us back to the question of how much you should charge for your book.

When I first released my book I priced it at $3.99. Shortly afterward, I pushed it up to $4.99, and then I did a two-week-long $0.99 sale. None of those strategies helped me sell a great number of books, so after conferring with my support group and checking out other books published by Indie authors, I settled on $3.99. The vast majority of books that I've sold have been priced at $3.99, and when I published the second book of my trilogy, *My Name Is Hardly*, I priced it at $4.99 and left my first book at the $3.99 level. This worked for a little while, but when I returned the price of *My Name Is Hardly* to $3.99 the sales became more consistent. So, today that's where it stays.

You'll find the majority of novels by Indie authors priced from $2.99 to $6.99. Novellas are priced lower and nonfiction books are priced higher, and sell at the higher price. I have a friend whose first book, a nonfiction book, performs best at $6.99. No matter where he's tried pricing his book, he still sells more at this price point than anywhere else.

I went through an interesting exercise when I released my collection of short stories. ***Lies I Never Told-A Collection of Short Stories*** is indeed a short collection; it's only about twenty thousand words. It contains four previously unpublished stories, a story that was published by an online magazine, and the first chapters of my two novels. My intention was to try to get as many copies out as possible, introduce new readers to my work, and give my existing readers some new material to read.

I enrolled my book in Amazon's KDP Select because that's where I've been successful, and I'd like to continue to support the program, so my pricing options were somewhat limited. I didn't want to give it away for free continuously; I had to charge at least $0.99. My thoughts were that I didn't necessarily need to make money on this book. I'd like to recoup my expenses (editing, cover design, formatting et cetera), but my intention is to use this book to promote my other work and get my name out there. If I could, I'd give it away for free all the time, but as a participant in KDPS I can't; I need to charge $0.99. So I did. Except a funny thing happened. At that price it didn't sell. I initially sold quite a few copies to my readers, who were waiting for a new release from me, but then it stalled, and I mean stalled. So, I ran all of my free days and gave away a few thousand copies. Then I put it back to $0.99 and it still didn't sell. So I raised it to $2.49, and I started to sell some e-books. For six months it worked. I sold a few books here and there, but once again it stalled. So, again, I dropped the price to $0.99, and again, it began to sell. Currently $0.99 seems to be the magic number for this book, but it seems to change every few months. Although I'm reluctant to price it above $0.99 because it is a short collection and includes previously published material, the market will dictate where it should be priced, and to this point, no one has returned the book. (Amazon has a system in place where readers can return an e-book if they've ordered it in error or change their minds.)

Experiment, watch your results, make sure you wait a week or two before immediately making a price change, and when you find your sweet spot, leave it there because that's what readers are willing to pay for your work. We'll talk more about reduced sale pricing and of course giveaways later, but in terms of your regular price, that is, the price you're comfortable offering your work to readers for—once you've got it, keep it.

You also have the ability to price your books that are sold in other markets (UK, Canada, Europe, Japan, and Brazil) at other price points, to a certain extent. For example, if you're within the 70% royalty range (which for a full-length book is where you should be), you can price your book in the US at $3.99 and your book in the UK at the equivalent of $2.99 (the lowest allowable under the 70% rate). This allows you to price lower in markets where you may not be performing as strongly while keeping your price at your sweet spot in the largest market: the US.

When I speak at writers groups I'm often asked about pricing. There's usually a couple of authors in the group who feel they have a book that is so unique (usually it's nonfiction), and contains information that can't be accessed anywhere else, that the price of their books should be at least $9.99. I direct them to Amazon's pages and suggest they research their competition. I suggest that they find a book in their genre written by an author who is as well-known as they are and compare prices. Then check the author's rankings and see how well the book is selling. The objective is to find a book that is in your category, performing well, written by an author who is self-published like yourself. That's your competition. The optimistic authors from the writers group often directs me to books that are priced in the upper echelons and argues that the uniqueness of their material and the research that's been involved in compiling it is worth at least $9.99. I disagree. The majority of us are new authors building our reader base. We want to connect with lots of readers and get our work out there. Price competitively and aim high. Check out the other books on Amazon's site and price yourself at the same level. If you don't—if your prices vary from everyone else's, no matter what the subject matter, you won't even be in the game.

E-book prices are a bargain. There is some terrific literature available for a few dollars per book. I know this because I buy lots of books, and I often find great deals. Later in the book I'm going to talk about my experiences with Kindle Scout when Amazon published my new book. They priced *The Dead List* at $2.99. And it's sold very well. The books they publish through their more well-known in house publishing companies are priced in the $4.99 to $6.99 range. That's interesting information to draw from. I believe that your first book or two should be priced in that lower range, $2.99 to $3.99, but as we develop a reader base and our work becomes better known, I think we can nudge that number up to $4.99 or for a bestselling novel, perhaps even $5.99. Beyond that, it becomes expensive for some folks, but if you consider $2.99 to $3.99 as price points for your first two books and then add a dollar or two for your next releases (if you're successful, selling books, and building a readership), I don't think you can go wrong.

4.   Product Page

Once your book goes live on Amazon two things will happen. You'll be able to log in to your KDP dashboard and check your sales, and you'll be able to browse Amazon's website, type in your name or book title and find your book on its very own product page. This is a great feeling. After all the hours of creating, formulating, writing, editing, revising, and all the other tasks that you've done, your work is now available to readers all over the world. Yes, everywhere, because when you log in to your dashboard, you'll see that your book is for sale not only in the US, but also the United Kingdom, Germany, France, Spain, Italy, Canada, Japan, India, Brazil, Mexico, Netherlands, and Australia. Not only will you have a product page on **www.amazon.com,** you'll also have it on the other sites too. You'll be on **www.amazon.co.uk**, **www.amazon.de**, **www.amazon.ca**, and all the others.

Your product page will include a book description. This is where you'll see the synopsis you worked on earlier and submitted just before you uploaded your book. It'll also have an "Editorial Reviews" and "Author Bio" section. We'll work on these in a moment when we tackle Author

Central. Your product page will also show your overall ranking.

After checking your sales on your dashboard, the first place you'll probably go afterward is your product page to check your ranking, and at first you'll do it frequently. That's when your eyes will start to go a little square from all of the constant checking (or mine did anyway). You'll also notice that once you begin climbing to the top of your chosen category, it'll list your ranking in that category under your product description. And then, believe it or not, as your book gains momentum and readers start talking about it, there's even a discussion area at the bottom of the page where you'll see readers talking about your book. Plus, after you add your book to Goodreads (which we'll speak about next), there is a section where readers will describe your characters, book settings, and other specifics that you've written about.

Your product page is also where readers will be able to look inside your book and decide whether they wish to purchase it. We spoke about this earlier, and again, this is a great tool to showcase your work, so make sure when you get to the upload stage, you enable the "Look Inside" feature.

Familiarize yourself with your product page. Remember, you're the boss, you own your own business, and if something needs to be changed or tweaked, you can do it relatively quickly. If you choose to change your pricing or categories or rewrite your synopsis, you can do it and see the changes on this page. If the indent on a paragraph in your synopsis looks incorrect, nobody is going to change it. Again, you have to be aware of how your product looks to the public and change it yourself. Amazon isn't the publisher, you are; they are only distributing your product. Keep your eyes on your product page, and if changes need to be made, make them quickly.

5. Goodreads

If I have one regret in life, it's that I didn't spent more time utilizing Goodreads. Actually, that's not true. I have a couple of regrets in my life but, although it sounds like it from time to time, this book is not the story of my life. It's a guide to help you publish your book in a professional and efficient manner. In order to do that, we're going to learn more about Goodreads.

Goodreads is a readers site where readers can set up a virtual bookshelf, include the books they've read or are reading, review and comment on books, and interact with other readers. We sometimes ask, "Where are all the readers?" This is one of the places where you can find them.

Some of the forums and chat areas we've mentioned throughout this book are not necessarily author friendly. They all have areas where authors can post and comment, but as an author, you dare not enter into the readers-only areas, because those areas are reserved for people who want to objectively talk about the books they're reading. This is a good idea. I applaud the fact that there are heavily policed online areas, and they haven't turned into sites filled with blatant promotions.

Although Goodreads is fairly author friendly, it's designed for readers. This is a site for book lovers and readers. Shortly after I published each of my first two books, I entered their information into the Goodreads system and uploaded my cover and synopsis, and afterward, readers posted reviews. With my short-story collection, I was slow to enter it and a reader beat me to the punch and entered the details. As an author on Goodreads you have the ability to create discussion groups that your readers can participate in, you can have giveaways and promotions, and you can create lists of books that are similar to yours. It's a great way to interact with the people who are reading your work or are looking for books like yours, but remember to tread carefully – the mandate of this site is to help readers interact with other readers.

Currently I don't have a strong presence on Goodreads. Again, this goes back to balance. You can only spend so much time on social networks promoting your work, and the majority of our time should be spent writing. Goodreads is a place where I haven't spent a great deal of time, and perhaps I should have. I should have done this because Amazon now owns Goodreads. While they have said they don't intend to alter Goodreads in any way, just the fact that they now own the site and have access to all those readers makes me want to become a little more involved. So, if

Facebook is the network where you primarily spend your time interacting with readers, I'd suggest you consider Goodreads as your second outlet. This is where the real readers are, and now that they're part of the Amazon family, they've become even more important.

Amazon made life a little simpler for us at the beginning of 2016. Shelfari was also an Amazon-owned company, and their mandate was similar to Goodreads'. The two companies merged in February 2016. This means we no longer have to enter our book information in Shelfari as well as Goodreads. Previously when we entered our book information on Shelfari's site, it would show up on our product page. Suddenly Goodreads has become even more important. Already there is a relationship between the review system on your Amazon product page and the reviews posted on Goodreads. At some point I believe Goodreads and Amazon reviews will be merged. Remember, the next time you wonder where your readers are, look no farther than Goodreads.

6.   Author Central

Soon you'll be able to call yourself a published author. You'll have uploaded your book into the Kindle Direct Publishing system, and your book will be available for sale on Amazon's website. People you don't know will be purchasing it, and you'll receive reviews from far and wide. Shortly after I released my first book I even received a review from someone in Luxembourg. People all over the world will have access to your work. One of the things we've been doing throughout this book is branding. You may not realize it, but you are a brand and it's important to build that brand. Author Central allows you to do this. It lets you tell your readers who you are and what you're all about. Again, this is another of Amazon's tools that will help broaden your reach.

The first thing you need to do when you log in to Author Central at **www.authorcentral.amazon.com** is claim your book. Search for your book title and when the system asks whether you're the author, acknowledge that you are. Then, once that's been established, you can enter your details.

This is where you'll enter information into the "Editorial Reviews" and "About the Author" sections, and they'll be displayed on your book's product page. Bear in mind this, again, is one of the windows through which potential readers will examine your work. Ideally you want readers to be attracted to your cover and click on the thumbnail. Then, when they're directed to your product page, the synopsis hopefully is enough to entice them to purchase, but if not, the editorial reviews might do the trick. And, if that doesn't do it, perhaps they'll still be intrigued enough to click on your book cover and the "Look Inside" feature to learn more. Again, we're trying to cover as much ground as possible, and if there is a section that calls for information to be submitted, do it. The wider you spread your wings, the more likely you are to find potential readers.

Amazon offers you two opportunities to enter your book's synopsis. You can enter the information in the Book Description area of Author Central or in the KDP upload area. And, you can change the information as often as you like. The turnaround time to make changes seems to be faster through Author Central. If I want to make changes to my product description through Author Central it typically takes a few hours for the changes to show up on my product page. If I want to do it through KDP it can sometimes take a couple of days for the same changes to show up. In order to make a quick change and tweak, or adjust to the ever-changing marketplace, you can do it far quicker through Author Central.

For example, during the Christmas season I include this heading on my product description: Recommended Christmas Gift. I entered it under the "Book Review" section on Author Central. It showed up on my page less than an hour later. So, I was able to pop that enticing little heading on there in mid-December and remove it after the holidays. From time to time I'll title my product page with "Temporary Price Reduction." When I do this I'm able to make immediate changes while a promotion is running and then change it back afterward almost immediately. Sometimes, I also highlight reviews that I'm especially proud of, and when I was awarded a *Book Readers Award Group* (B.R.A.G.) medallion, I inserted it into the text too. For me, the time factor is important, so I tend to enter my information through Author Central. Amazon has altered its system so that neither the KDP dashboard system nor Author Central will override each other. In other words, whichever area the information has been entered in most recently is where it will show up.

The first section of Author Central we'll deal with is Editorial Reviews. You can't enter information in Author Central until your book has been released, so by this point you'll have accumulated some reviews. As we mentioned previously, some of these will be reviews you've canvassed from your beta readers and reviewers from review sites that you've submitted to, and hopefully you've received a few from random readers too. That way, you'll have some reviews to pick from. Pick the best parts of your top reviews from all of these accumulated reviews and post them. Don't try to post the whole review. The attention span of the reader who's browsing your product page is short, so just include punchy phrases and then credit the reviewer.

Incidentally, I've found when posting onto the Author Central pages, it's best to use a program other than Microsoft Word to copy and paste from. Notepad works great but Word for some reason won't allow you to indent paragraphs and place text exactly where you want it. So pick blurbs from your best reviews, and if you have reviews from a recognized source, place those toward the top of the section. Don't go crazy listing reviews even if you have lots of them. Three or four is probably the maximum you want to show and only the best sections of the reviews should be displayed. There's no need to list reviews that detail your plot all over again; this is already in the synopsis further up the page. A good review blurb under Editorial Reviews should comment on the writing and how the story made the reviewer feel.

Your "About the Author" or bio section should be written in a certain format. The majority of Indie authors start by listing that they've been writing since they were children, and then they talk about the imaginary voices that they're now bringing to life, and finally they mention the work itself. Save those types of self-indulgent comments for interviews once you've hit the bestseller lists. Remember these rules when writing your professional author bio: write in the third person, use your full name, begin with awards and experience, list your body of works, and, finally, include a couple of personal details.

The encyclopedia of effective author bios is at your fingertips. By this point you're following the blogs of successful authors; you may even have "friended" some of them on Facebook or are trading tweets on Twitter. Study their bios (if they are indeed selling books). You'll find some are quirky and inject humor into their personal bios. I've found that as a new author, it's difficult to get away with humor unless you're very, very funny. Once you've built a following you might be able to do it, but my suggestion would be that as an initial bio, keep it professional and accessible. If you follow the guideline above—third person, full name, awards and accolades, and brief personal details—you can't go wrong.

And, finally, make sure you link your blog and Twitter account to your Author Central page. Author Central is like having your own website without any of the costs involved. I have a website. I purchased the domain martincrosbie.com before I released my first book. After neglecting it for a little while and concentrating on Author Central, I decided to put more effort into it and it has paid off. I detail those efforts in Chapter Eleven – The Business of Writing. While I was in in-between mode, I directed traffic to my Author Central page. Again, it's almost like having your own personal website without the expense, and it's very easy to maintain. I've linked my blog (from my website) and Twitter feed there too. Plus there's a section where you can list your upcoming events. So, if you have a sale on one of your books, a new release, or a book-signing event, let your readers know. Author Central lists your bio, your books, your events, and your Twitter feed, all on one page. Author Central has some limitations, but it's still a very important tool that you should be taking advantage of.

7. Amazon Affiliate Program

Amazon has a program that will pay you a commission on books and other items that you sell. This is in addition to royalties you'll receive when readers purchase your books. You're going to post and promote links to your books and others in many different places online. You'll post them on your website (if you have one), as well as Facebook, Twitter, and any other forums or groups you frequent. By joining the Amazon affiliate program, you'll be able to monetize these links.

When you sign up to become an Amazon affiliate, right here, **https://affiliate-program.amazon.com/,** Amazon will provide you with a unique link for your books that has your affiliate identity embedded into the link. Then, when someone clicks on the link and purchases your book, you're given a small commission for directing traffic to Amazon's site. Additionally, if they purchase other products you're given a commission on those sales also. It's advantageous for you to become an Amazon affiliate and post the unique link everywhere you can. There really is no downside. K.S. Brooks is an expert at writing tutorials, and she gives excellent guidance right here on how to monetize your links:

www.indiesunlimited.com/2012/06/12/amazon-com-monetize-tutorial

If you find this information useful, K.S. would love to hear from you. The contact information for K.S., and all the other authors who kindly allowed their charts and blogs to be shared with you, is at the bottom of their articles.

8. CreateSpace

So far, we've talked primarily about e-books, but one of the suggestions made to me, when I couldn't find any traction and I was having trouble selling books, was to produce a print copy of *My Temporary Life*. This was a really good idea and much easier to accomplish than I could ever have imagined. To date I've sold several thousand print books, and although my e-book sales have far exceeded that number, it's still hundreds of people who have reached into their pockets and bought my book, and for that I'm very grateful.

CreateSpace is an Amazon company, but instead of being in Seattle (Amazon's corporate headquarters), they're in Las Vegas. I've produced a print copy of all of my novels with the exception of my short story collection. It's a shorter book, and I don't believe there'd be enough value for the reader. The experience I've had with CreateSpace has been fantastic. They have an extremely user-friendly system; if you follow their step-by-step process, you can have a print copy of your book sitting in front of you within days. The first step is to upload covers, your manuscript, pricing information, and basically all of the other things you've dealt with as you've been publishing your e-book. Basically, you're just transferring the information to another outlet. The only real difference is that once you've uploaded your Microsoft Word document into their system, you can view what your book will look like on their previewer. If, like myself, you're using a professional cover designer, make sure he furnishes you with an image for your Kindle e-book as well as print book. The print book requires a spine and back cover. And, if you want to stick with the pros, you can have your formatter create a CreateSpace formatted file also. In keeping with my mandate of attempting to produce professional material, I rely on my formatter and cover designer for CreateSpace also. The difference in cost is minimal, it frees you up to do other things, and it's always nice to have a professional working for you.

Once you're happy with it, you should order a proof and have a good, long look at the proof once it arrives. If you're satisfied with the product, then go ahead and order some print books. Make sure your print release coincides with your e-book release. We're going to discuss the importance of your launch and how important the first thirty days are in the next chapter, so it's always a good idea to have your print book either go live at the same time as your e-book or slightly afterward.

CreateSpace has an Expanded Distribution feature that will allow you to have your book available through wholesalers. Until the end of 2013 this was a paid feature. It's now available for free. Make sure you take advantage of it. Expanded Distribution will help get your book into bookstores. There is a nasty rumor that circulates from time to time. Claims are sometimes made that self-published books cannot be sold in bookstores. I'm happy to help dispel this myth, and it truly is a myth. My books are currently available in a number of brick and mortar bookstores including Powell's in Portland, Oregon, the largest bookstore in the world. I detail how I canvassed stores to add my books to their inventories and how I arranged book signings in Chapter Ten – More Promotions.

With the Expanded Distribution feature, bookstores can order directly from their wholesalers. This is a bonus for you and again, it's free, so make sure you take advantage of it.

Be careful how you price your print books. CreateSpace gives you a minimum allowable price. I reached a point in summer of 2013 where I wasn't selling many print books, so I lowered the pricing on one of my books as low as they'd let me. So, instead of my usual $12.99 in North America I was $10.99. I also lowered it through their Expanded Distribution feature. As mentioned, this is where wholesalers can buy your book for different markets. After lowering my pricing I immediately sold three books through the Expanded Distribution feature and my royalty payment was -$0.30. Yes, that is a negative amount.

After several emails back and forth with CreateSpace this was the response I received:

Our Lead Team has confirmed that you purchased Expanded Distribution in January 2012. This means that when you set your list price, the royalty amount due to you was visible within the pricing step of the project homepage. As this is not a royalty error on our side, we cannot make an adjustment to your royalties.

I apologize for any inconvenience this information has presented.

Furthermore, I have passed along your feedback regarding our system that should not allow titles to go available with negative royalties being possible. We appreciate your comments, and we look forward to continuing to improve our offerings in order to better serve you.

My concern wasn't the negative amount. I can live with that, although I should be paid something for my books. My real concern was that this is a glitch in their system. Their minimum allowable amount should be pre-set at a level that will allow authors to be paid for their books. It isn't. Needless to say I did raise my pricing so this wouldn't happen again. The system has still not been fixed. So, make sure your pricing is set at a level where you'll be paid royalties. If the estimated royalty payment is less than $0.60, I would suggest you raise it. Since I've changed mine I've always been in a positive payment position.

As you can see, it really doesn't cost you anything to release a print book, so there's no reason not to do it, and some readers still prefer a paper copy. I've used my print books as prizes in contests, plus when I attend conferences and writers fairs I always have my print books on display. It's an important part of the dream too, isn't it? I don't know about you, but when I imagined myself writing books, I could actually see the book and hold it, and by publishing through CreateSpace, you can do that. This is another way of taking advantage of one of Amazon's tools.

Those are the main tools that Amazon offers. You'll alter, tweak, radically change and become frustrated with them from time to time. Now, unfortunately, I have some bad news for you. Just when you thought all this time-taxing work on Author Central was over, it isn't. If you have published a print book through CreateSpace, you need to enter the information all over again for the print version. This is where copying and pasting from Notepad can be an advantage. You'll notice on the upper right hand section of your Author Central page there is an area where you can click on either your print or Kindle version. You need to manually enter each one. The information won't cross over on its own. There's an Author Central section on some of the non-US Amazon sites, and you have to enter your information there too. There aren't as many sections on the non-US sites, so it won't take you quite as long. The information on each of the foreign sites isn't in English of course, but the format is the same. You can have the US page open and follow those directions to enter your information on the foreign pages. Keep your eye on the other Author Central sites, because Amazon expands them from time to time, and sooner or later you'll be able to enter your information—and spread your reach—to all of them, all over the world.

CHAPTER SEVEN HOMEWORK

1. Do your research and then pick two categories that are applicable to your book. One a popular, populous, genre and another that you feel is winnable.

2. Pick keywords, lots of them. You'll need them when you initially upload your book, but you'll need them again from time to time when you enter your information on different promotional sites. Keep a document ongoing with lists of keywords and (by referencing the chart) make sure your words have been used recently and are broad in terms of popularity.

3. Find your pricing sweet spot. Search other self-published books in your genre and find a price for your book that's between $2.99 and $9.99 and remember, readers are taking a chance on a new author; keep the pricing accessible.

4. Familiarize yourself with your product page, those of others you're competing against, and the product pages of other authors in your support group. If one of your confidantes' rankings jumps up overnight, you want to know about it and what caused it.

5. Join Goodreads and participate as a reader and author, and submit your information in every area that's offered to you. All it takes is one or two readers to find your work, leave positive reviews, and help spread word about your book.

6. Enter your information into Author Central, remembering to enter again if you have a print and Kindle version and again on the non-US sites also.

7. Become an Amazon affiliate and receive your unique link so you can receive commission on traffic that you drive to their site. You're a self-employed author with your own business, and there's no reason you can't run your career like a business.

CHAPTER SIX FOLLOW-UP

1. Do you have lots of reviewers and beta readers lined up who have read and reviewed your book and are waiting to post a review on Amazon and Goodreads? If not, submit some more. Reviews are going be very important in the next chapter.

2. Are you familiarizing yourself with the protocol in different groups and forums? Do you know who the workhorses are in terms of supporting others? Do you have a relationship with the

administrators of the sites?

3. Are you receiving alerts from Google and Mention? If not, add additional search words.

4. Repeat #1. Keep seeking out reviews. You can never have too many.

CHAPTER EIGHT
PLANNING AND EXECUTING
A SUCCESSFUL BOOK LAUNCH
Or
Ships Don't Just Disappear in the Night, Do They?

Yes, they do disappear. Just ask 10CC, the band that wrote "Ships Don't Just Disappear in the Night." They disappeared (kind of), and books do too. Fortunately, you can resurrect them. You can start all over again and take another stab, but if you're going to do this right, and remember, doing it right means taking a professional and efficient approach to *this*, and *this* is your business, then you need to have a book launch planned in advance of hitting the upload button. Too often we're in such a rush to get our books out there because we're still in that "world needing to recognize our brilliance" stage and we launch too quickly. Your launch is about building momentum, maintaining it, and being prepared to adjust your strategy. I'm going to break down your launch into several parts; some take place before your release and some are during.

1. **Reviews and Reviewers**
2. **Pre-Order**
3. **Blog Tours**
4. **Podcasts and Interviews**
5. **Newspapers and Magazines**
6. **Tweaking**

1. Reviews and Reviewers

We've talked about how important reviewers are already, but we're going to revisit them. The key thing to remember once again is that we're trying to spread our wings as wide as we can. We want our names and book titles to be in as many places as possible. We can write guest blogs and do online interviews and post on Facebook and tweet till the cows come home but really, there's only one place we truly want to be. We want to be where the readers are looking for books, and that's primarily on Amazon's site. Amazon has a "Hot New Releases" category. It should be your goal to get on this list and stay there for as long as possible. Your book is only valid for inclusion on this list for thirty days from your release date, and to get on there you need to sell books, and to sell books you need reviews. And to get reviews you need readers to read your book and then post a review.

In order for readers to post their review on Amazon's site, they need to have purchased your book or purchased product from Amazon equaling or exceeding a set dollar amount. That dollar amount seems to be a secret. Amazon won't disclose how much a reader needs to spend with them in order to post a review. So, ideally, you need to have had readers (who are Amazon customers), read your book before it's released, and if you followed the guidelines in Chapter Six, you should have your beta readers and a number of reviewers ready to post as soon as your book goes live.

Some of my best friends are reviewers. Really, they are. I've formed some very close friendships with reviewers since releasing my first book. I think one of the reasons I have an affinity with reviewers is that they look at e-books and e-book marketing and presentation in the same way I do. They see the incorrect ways that authors sometimes approach it and they don't like it. They have authors send them their work in the wrong formats (I've done this), authors solicit their review without exercising the correct protocol (I've done this too), and authors ask the reviewer to do all the work promoting their book (fortunately, I haven't done this).

Most reviewers don't get paid. Reviewers write blogs and reviews because they have a genuine love of finding new literature. Years ago, when I was a young man, flipping through LPs in the record store (yes, that long ago), my goal was to find a band or a song that no one had heard of that would make a difference. From time to time I did it, too. I'd find a sound that took me from where I was and put me somewhere else. It was a sound that made a difference, and to find it meant everything to me. Reviewers do the same thing. They want to find that talent, or story, and they want to help share it with the world. Unfortunately, along the way, they're going to find a lot of books that miss, and it's their responsibility to let their followers know that the book hasn't hit its target. It's what they have to do.

You're going to receive good reviews and not-so-good reviews. I've had both as well as everything in between. You need to get used to all of them. I'd love to have more five-star reviews, but readers and reviewers are entitled to their opinions. If they're going to take a chance and read my book and then take the time to post a review I have to respect that.

Previous to your launch, it's very important to get your book out to as many readers as you can. You may want to enlist the help of your friends and family and ask them to post an honest review too. I've found the best way to do this is to tell my friends and family that I'm trying to become a better writer and please don't be afraid to tell me what you really think. I believe in my work, and I know you believe in yours too. We've come to the point where we're going to let the world see what has been going on in our heads for the past few months or years and we're going to discover their honest reactions. And, based on my experience, I can guarantee you that family and friends will not automatically give you positive reviews. Sometimes they can be our harshest critics. There's a biblical saying: "No prophet is accepted in his own hometown." I tend to think that sometimes friends and family set the bar a little higher when appraising our work. Nevertheless, we want to become better writers and have to be open to criticism.

If you're struggling to find reviewers, there are Facebook groups that are populated by members who are looking for books to review. In the search bar type "reviewers" or "book reviewers" and you'll find a number of different groups. You'll find that most of these groups work well, but the completion rate isn't as high as dealing with a professional reviewer.

Sometimes your book will be shuffled to the bottom of their "to be read" lists, and it can take a while before you see any results, but sometimes you have to rely on the percentages. There's an old saying in sales: "If you throw enough crap against the wall, some of it will stick." The same can be applied to submitting to reviewers through Facebook groups. Some of them will indeed review your book, and some of the most insightful reviews I've had have come from random readers who found me through Facebook. You never know; you just have to keep submitting.

The idea is to get as many potential reviewers ready to go so that once your book is released you can politely let them know and ask them to please post a review on Amazon's site. Bear in mind that not all of your reviewers and beta readers will be from the US. Some will be from the UK or Canada or even further afield. Reviews are important on all of Amazon's sites, but it's important to ask them to re-post their reviews on the US site also. You may find that the majority of your books sell in the UK or another market but typically, the majority of readers, or buyers, are in the US. It's the largest market, so we want to focus there.

In the Helpful Links list you'll find lists of dozens of review sites. Remember to follow their submission guidelines.

2. Pre-Order

In late 2014 Amazon gave all authors the capability of offering their books to readers as a pre-order.

This can help build serious momentum, and you can hit the ground running when you launch. Your product page is displayed during the pre-order period, and readers can order your book. No payment is taken from the reader until your book goes live. You will see your rankings displayed during the pre-order time. At the end of 2015 Jennifer Skutelsky's very fine book was offered as a pre-order. It hit the top five overall on Amazon's rankings, prior to release. According to Theresa Ragan's chart, that means Jennifer was selling approximately three thousand books each day. That's a lot of momentum. Your pre-order can begin any time up to three months before your release. You will also be asked to provide a launch date. The final copy of your file must be uploaded into the system ten days before this date. That deadline is written in stone. If you decide to offer your book as a pre-order, check out Laurie Boris's tutorial right here:

www.indiesunlimited.com/2014/09/02/amazonpreorder/.

3. Blog Tours

Although blogging seems to have lost some of its effectiveness in terms of connecting with new readers there are still authors who manage to run successful blog tours. Like so many things when it comes to a promotion, it often depends on "where" and "when" they take place.

Blog tours are pre-determined daily stops where you post a blog on different sites. There are promotional companies that can set these up for you, and some of them are very effective at finding the most popular sites for you to post on. Or, you can network with site owners and query them yourself. If you're following our guidelines, then blog opportunities are probably coming your way by now, and you shouldn't have to search out too many places to query.

Blogging is work that sometimes could be better spent writing new material, but it's also writing practice. It shows the reader what type of writer you are, so it's hard to argue against blogging. As part of your pre-launch strategy, you should have some blogs already written. Make sure your blogs are interesting and remember, readers are only interested in your personal details if they truly are interesting (bordering on remarkable is a good guideline to abide by). Once you achieve a certain level of success, there will be more interest in the name of your dog when you were nine or the reason you never tried out for band in high school, but for now, treat blogging the same way you'd write your book. Write things that readers will want to read.

I facilitate an annual "12 Blogs of Christmas" group promotion, and I'll usually guest blog anywhere that I'm invited. If it's a small site, large site, site with only three followers, I don't care. I feel that if I'm invited, if you want to have my words on your page, then I'll do it. Because of this I've blogged all over the place. When we reach Chapter Twelve—Finding a Balance I'll show you how you can find time to write and even accumulate blogs. This way when an opportunity is presented, you'll be ready.

Time your blog tour to coincide with your book launch. You're going to press the upload button at the end of this chapter so get ready. Ideally you want to start your tour two or three days before your release date and continue for two or three weeks afterward. Remember, you want to be on Amazon's Hot New Releases list, and your book will only be eligible for thirty days after its release.

4. Podcasts and Interviews

I believe in podcasts. I think they're going to grow and grow in popularity. A podcast is a radio show broadcast over the Internet. It's usually broadcast live but can also be accessed and listened to afterward. There are hundreds of them available to you. I've been very fortunate. I've been interviewed by some of the best. I was on Ann White's *Creating Calm* network, Pam Stack's *Authors on the Air* show, and Cyrus Webb's *Conversations Live* show as well as several others. They're fun to do. You can sit in your living room and talk on the phone to someone who's usually a very good interviewer. Then, you can promote the show through your social networks. It's a great opportunity to relax and talk about writing and your work. Just remember, promote it before, during, and afterward. Tweet and Facebook the details and don't forget to mention it on your Author Central page, too, as a coming event. Let everybody know about your show and then relax and have fun with it.

A great source of podcasts is BlogTalkRadio. Here's the link: **www.blogtalkradio.com/.** If you type "authors" or "writers" into the search bar, you'll find lots of shows that feature writers just like yourself who have a book they want to talk about. Query them in the same professional manner you'd query reviewers. The other source, and this will happen organically, is again your support group. Others will pass along information on podcasts they've been invited to participate in, and you'll do the same.

You'll also have interview requests from other authors, Indie writer sites, and review sites. I enjoy doing interviews. The questions are sent to you in advance so you have time to formulate your responses and come up with answers that readers may enjoy reading. Remember, whether you're blogging or answering interview questions, treat it the same way you'd treat writing your book. You want to entertain the reader and entice them to keep reading or listening and hopefully it will encourage them to check out your work.

5. Newspapers and Magazines

In this section I'm referring to traditionally published print periodicals. And yes, they want to know what you've been up to. Once you've reached the point where you're working in conjunction with your support group and promoting your book in a constructive fashion online, it'll seem as though the whole world knows what's happening with self-publishing. This is incorrect. We tend to become so insulated we forget that the know-how we've acquired and the things we're doing on a daily basis aren't common knowledge. Most of the general public (and they're our potential audience), don't know what an Indie author is. A lot of them haven't even bought an e-reader device yet.

When I started selling lots of books, I tried to do my little bit to get the word out there. I wrote articles in the hopes that some of my local newspapers might print them. There's a lot of interest in self-publishing, and the majority of the general public aren't aware of what's happening with Amazon and e-books and the fact that authors have found a new way to connect with readers. I submitted articles on spec to several newspapers, and some of them printed my stories. Most of them don't pay you for your work, but it gives you an incredible opportunity to reach readers who aren't necessarily spending time online—they're still reading papers and magazines the traditional way. Some of the articles I wrote were still receiving feedback in their online forums (because quite often they're released online and in print), months after they were first published.

The other way to approach newspapers and magazines is to email a press release letting them know that you've self-published your book. You need to structure your press release so it's in the form of a story. Newspapers want to print something interesting, especially if it has a human-interest angle. Try to come up with a hook. Why are you writing? Other than the entertainment value they may receive, will anyone benefit from reading your book other than yourself? My story was interesting because I was rejected by so many traditional publishers and agents. Canada's *Globe and Mail* newspaper ran a full-page story on me (once I'd hit the bestseller lists) and called me a "traditional publishing reject." I keep meaning to have a T-shirt made up with "Traditional Publishing Reject" on it, but I haven't gotten around to it yet. Find a hook or an angle that'll be interesting to readers and approach editors and newspapers by telling them your story.

Smaller newspapers and magazines will tend to be more interested in your self-publishing experience than major dailies, but why not try anyway? You'll find templates for press releases online (again, try Googling it), or Microsoft Word has free templates too. Again, this is an instance where you should be doing it yourself. Don't pay someone to issue a press release for you. The editors' contact information is usually listed on the websites of the newspapers and magazines you plan to target. You have nothing to lose by emailing them. Getting some kind of mention anywhere in print, whether it's a full-page feature or a couple of lines in the local newspaper is valuable, and, other than your time, it costs you nothing.

6. Tweaking

Be prepared to make changes. If your sales stall after that initial buy from your family and friends be prepared to shift gears. There's still time to get on the Hot New Releases list.

Check out what's currently selling on Amazon. Which books are in the top fifty right now? Are the rankings primarily populated with romances and you've listed your suspense/romance under thrillers? If your book fits within this category, change it to contemporary romance. Are reviewers not posting your reviews fast enough? Hit up a Facebook review site group and tell them your dilemma. Let them know that you need honest reviews immediately and ask for help. Are your keywords not producing? Check out the list of the most recently used popular keywords and change yours. The whole idea is to find some momentum and then try to maintain your sales level by finding ways to get your name and book in front of readers, and sometimes that requires a little tweaking.

From all the newspaper stories, blogs, podcasts, and interviews that I've had the honor of participating in, other opportunities almost always appeared. The most unlikely promotional opportunities have often led to other things for me. From a newspaper article I wrote, I was invited to speak at writers groups and a conference. When I spoke at the conference, I was invited to speak at a library. And, when I spoke at the library, I was invited to teach a course on self-publishing. It goes on and on and before you know it, you've become a brand, and you're being referred to as a self-publishing expert. More importantly, readers are reading your book. It doesn't take long. At the end of 2011 nobody was interested in hearing me speak and now I have the luxury of declining speaking engagements (in order to keep writing).

After your initial thirty days are up, we're going to start promoting in earnest, and we'll talk about that in the next chapter. Our homework for this chapter is below, and as you can see we're now at the serious stage. This is where theory-time is over and you're going to release your book. Congratulations, you're now a self-published author—that's a great accomplishment!

CHAPTER EIGHT HOMEWORK

1. Upload your book to your platform of choice. Yes, it's time; go ahead and become a published author!
2. If you're signing up for KDP Select, make sure you tick the appropriate box and commit to the ninety-day enrollment.
3. Purchase an e-book copy yourself and examine it for any formatting flaws, problems with your cover, or even that glaring editorial error everyone has overlooked. If it looks okay don't worry, but if there's a problem, correct it, have your formatter reformat (hopefully at no, or minimal cost) and re-upload.
4. Release your print book through CreateSpace and their Expanded Distribution network. Purchase a copy and go through the same

checks that you did above in #3.

5. Alert your reviewers and beta readers that your book is live and that you're ready to have those reviews posted.
6. Hit the virtual road. Start blogging, interacting on the threads where your interviews are posted, and contributing in forums and groups.
7. In the cold light of day, have a closer look at your product page, including your synopsis and Author Central details. Tweak or change completely if necessary.

CHAPTER SEVEN FOLLOW-UP

1. Using Theresa Ragan's chart, check how the top books are performing in the two categories you've chosen. Do you feel that you're going to be able to compete against them?
2. Are you continuing to monitor your product page? Do you feel that your keywords are bringing readers to your book? Is your pricing competitive with similar books? If not, make the changes.
3. Have you entered your information into Goodreads and Author Central? Your book is live now, so you need to spend a few hours doing the work, and you should do it as soon as you possibly can.
4. Have you become an Amazon affiliate? This is another source of revenue for you. Once the additional work is done, there's very little effort involved, so there's no reason not to do it.

CHAPTER NINE
FREE AND DISCOUNTED PROMOTIONS
Or
What Happens When You Stop Making Sense?

Without the opportunity I had with KDP Select to give away my book, I wouldn't have reached the levels of success that I have. As previously mentioned, when you enroll in Amazon's KDP Select program for three months you're entitled to some benefits—you're eligible to be paid on borrows from the Kindle Owners' Lending Library, your book is available to subscribers in the Kindle Unlimited program, you can participate in a Kindle Countdown Deal (I'll expand on this in a moment), and you have the ability to give away your book for up to five days. In February of 2012 I gave away my book for three days. Fifty thousand readers downloaded it. Every time I refreshed my KDP dashboard the numbers spiked upward. And then, on the Monday morning when my book returned as a paid sale, I sold seven hundred books. On the Tuesday, I sold two thousand and on the Wednesday I sold three thousand e-books. This was the month when I made over $46,000. The previous month, on all platforms (I was still published through Smashwords at that time), I made less than $500.

During this time I was able to look at Amazon's overall bestseller rankings and see my book listed in the top ten. At one point I was between one of *The Hunger Games* books and one of the *Twilight* books in paid sales. I still can't believe that I sold three thousand books in one day. It was a mind-numbing time, and, without trying to sound too dramatic, afterward nothing was ever quite the same.

Because I was able to find so many readers for my book (paid and free), I was contacted by Amazon. They told me they were going to mention me in a press release and asked whether I'd allow them to disclose my earnings. The story for them was that previous to enrolling with KDP

Select, I had made less than $500, but with KDP Select I'd made much more than that in just one month. After some thought, I allowed them to publicize the amount, and that's when the craziness really began. *Publisher's Weekly* mentioned me, television stations in North America and the UK talked about my book, *Forbes* magazine interviewed me, and I received notifications (through Mention.com and Google Alerts) that media outlets around the world were talking about my book and my self-publishing story. In a moment I'll explain how this all happened (including the fortuitous aspect of it), but for now I'd like to tell you what it *felt* like when it happened.

I hope you have to deal with this same situation, or a situation that's even more beyond what you could ever have imagined. To say it was incredible isn't giving enough life or power to how it felt at the time. It really came from nowhere, and to be able to brag that I arguably had the most downloaded e-book in North America for one weekend was, and is, something I still can't wrap my head around. And then, to reach so many readers and sell so many books afterward truly was a gift. All I'd ever wanted was for people to read my book, and boy, oh boy, did I ever get that.

One of my passions is running. I run long distances with a group of friends, and when my book became a bestseller I was training for my first marathon. I'd run several half marathons but hadn't run twenty-six miles (forty-two kilometers) yet. So, in addition to promoting my book, learning about self-publishing, trying to produce new material, and working at my day job, I was typically running twenty-five to thirty miles a week, training for my race. Yes, you're right, there was little time for sleep, but somehow I was managing. I'm stubborn, and the best motivator for me is when someone tells me I can't do something. I love it. When I received all those rejection letters, I printed them up and taped them all over my walls. I could feel it every day. I could feel myself being pushed to show all those letter-writers they were wrong. So, needless to say, if I'm training for a race, it's going to take a lot for me to give up. I did though. I stopped training for my marathon.

I was in the midst of running a thirteen-mile (twenty-one kilometer) training route one Sunday. My book was sitting in the #2 position in the Romantic/Suspense category, I'd made more money in one month than I could ever have imagined, I was receiving interview requests from all over the world, I was receiving messages and emails from readers every day, and I was mentally and physically exhausted. I stopped running and got a ride home. I had to. I sat on my couch and realized I hadn't stopped in a long time. Most of my time for the past two years had been spent sitting in front of a computer, and I'd been so focused on making all the correct decisions that I hadn't done anything else in a long time. So I dropped my training schedule back and decided that a marathon would have to wait. I still concentrated on training for half-marathons, but I just didn't have the time, energy, or mental faculties to do everything else. It was a good decision. Either way I was going to stop, but at least this way I stopped under my own steam. Oh, and by the way, I did run that marathon. I did it about a year later. As I said, I don't like to be told that I can't do something.

After my first free run, I sold more books than I could ever have imagined selling. I was lucky. I'd had help and I'd worked hard to present a professional product that I thought readers would enjoy, and my timing was impeccable. At that time, in February 2012, after giving away fifty thousand e-books, when I moved back as a paid sale, Amazon's computers credited my book in their system as the equivalent of one-tenth of fifty thousand paid sales. It shot up the rankings and stayed there for quite some time, enabling me to sell a lot of books. Beginning the next month, in March 2012, they began to change their system. Today, it's arguable whether Amazon awards any credits for free downloads. So, the post-free sales spike that so many of us enjoyed is difficult to replicate, and it's become much more difficult to do what I, and others, did. It can still work, but the authors who are currently successful with free promotions tend to have a series of linked books.

In early 2013 Joe Konrath wrote a blog post detailing how his last free promotions helped him earn $100,000 in six weeks. Nope, my editor didn't miss an error; I wrote that correctly. He made $100,000 in six weeks. Joe is a popular writer and has a large catalog of books, and his sales were spurred by a free promotion that he ran. So, for Joe, who was one of the first authors to give away his books, this type of promotion still yielded rewards. He sees peripheral sales of his other books during his sale and a rise in sales of the featured book afterward. Unfortunately, the numbers today are lower. You can still give away tens of thousands of e-books, but the sales afterward aren't as strong.

I ran other free promotions after my initial "hitting it out of the park" promo, but none of them were as successful as the first one, and none have been as successful as Joe's. The last couple of free promotions I've run have allowed me to reach a lot of readers, but they have not translated into a great number of paid sales. I need more content, and I need books that are in a series and linked together on my product page.

The debate over the effectiveness of giving your book away for free is ongoing and probably always will be. A colleague and I often debate whether they still work. Every time I show him the results of an author giving away thousands of books and seeing virtually no return when the book is returned as a paid sale, he points to an example where an author earns $5,000 to $10,000 in royalties when his book returns to the regular price. And, when I check out the rankings, I confirm that he's right. Free promotions occasionally work, every day. It can still be done; the results just aren't as consistent as they were two years ago. There's an element of luck and timing, because you never know who is trying to reach the discretionary dollars of all those e-book buyers at the same time you are, but there will always be that same challenge. If you decide to run a KDP Select free promotion, go in with an open mind. Approach it with the intention of reaching a lot of readers, and if the sales spike happens afterward consider it a bonus. Recognize that free promotions are a tool to build your reader base and gain reviews and occasionally can be effective and work as a way to sell books.

From the outset of this book I told you the system has changed. The above paragraphs illustrate those changes. I'm now going to tell you what we did to combat this change. There really is no secret—discounted advertising, or selling your book at a reduced price for a limited time, became the most consistent way to reach a lot of readers. The best way to run a discounted promotion is with a Kindle Countdown Deal. As part of your KDP Select benefits, you can discount your book for up to five days as part of a Kindle Countdown Deal. Under normal circumstances, when you discount your price below $2.99 your royalty rate reverts to 35%. With a Countdown Deal you retain the 70% royalty rate for the period of your promotion (five days maximum). You can choose to reduce your pricing to $0.99 for the Countdown period or raise it incrementally from $0.99 back up to the retail price.

Below is a step-by-step guide to running either a successful free or discounted promotion. Remember, new sites come along from time to time and others become inactive. You currently have in your hands (or on your Kindle), what I believe to be the most current techniques available to help you connect with readers. This book is updated every twelve to eighteen months (and you'll receive the updated copy from Amazon), but remember, the best way to stay abreast of what's currently effective is to continue cultivating relationships with others in your support group and paying it forward as we've discussed. By doing this, the information on what's working and what isn't will come to you. And you'll be aware of the latest and best market strategies.

Although there are similarities in terms of how you will run your free and discounted promotions, I'm going to separate them for your convenience. If your eyes begin to go fuzzy from reading this information, skip it and go to the next chapter. You're going to utilize this section as a "how-to" when you run your free or discounted promotion. It details each step that you will take, and although it's important to know, it's not necessary to familiarize yourself with each detail until you're ready to run your promotion. Don't be discouraged; I'm going to show you how to establish balance between writing and non-writing activities later in the book. Trust me, it's all going to work out.

FREE PROMOTIONS
  1. **Pick Your Days**
  2. **Book Your Ads**
  3. **Social Network**

4. **Time Your Run**

5. **Cross Your Fingers**

1. Pick Your Days

This is one of the mysteries and one of the most asked questions by Indie authors. Which days are most effective in terms of giving away your e-book away as part of a KDP Select promotion? And should you run two days in a row, or three in a row, or all five at once? The answer is—like so many things about promotions—it depends. There are so many factors. You just have to pick your days and live with them. There are a couple of things you should be aware of though. Summer is slow. Winter is the strongest sales season, and fall and spring are pretty good too. Long weekends are not a good time to sell e-books, and if there's a major event happening, stay away from it.

I have a friend who was sure that Super Bowl weekend would be the perfect time to give away her e-book. She felt that because it was a cozy romantic mystery, there would be all kinds of non-football watchers curled up with their Kindles or on their computers. It didn't work. Stay away from any holiday weekends or holiday weeks. The exception is Christmas. Lots of readers receive new Kindle e-readers over the holidays, and they're anxious to fill them up. Just after Christmas is a good and bad time to promote. It's good because readers are active on their Kindles and there are thousands of new Kindle owners, and it's bad because it's an ultra-competitive time. Other authors have the same idea you have and are trying to find readers.

Picking the busiest days to run your promotion is difficult, but I'll give you my personal preferences. I prefer to run two or three days in a row as opposed to four or even all five at once, and if possible my preference is to include one weekend day as part of the free period. Ideally my sale would take place on a Thursday, Friday, and Saturday, and my book would return as a paid sale on Sunday, which is typically a strong day for sales. Although it's become more difficult (and I'm sure you're tired of hearing me say that the system has changed), we want to assume that there may be a sales bounce once your book goes back to the paid rankings and that you'll also receive peripheral sales from your other titles.

There is no magic here. Yes, there are some days that are slower than others, but even on those slow days, authors are selling or giving away thousands of books. The only day that seems to be consistently slow, week after week, is Friday. I'd advise against using Friday as one of your first paid days once your promo has ended. By the way, don't be afraid of Mondays. I've had Mondays where I've sold hundreds of e-books. And just to further complicate matters, Tuesdays are typically the days when traditional publishers introduce a new title. So, it's busy out there on Tuesdays.

As you can see, picking days is a bit of a gamble. The important thing is to pull out the calendar and stay away from national holidays and full-scale events.

2. Book Your Ads

The original main players—Pixel of Ink **www.pixelofink.com** and EreaderNewsToday **www.ereadernewstoday.com** – are still effective in terms of spreading the words about your book, but their reach has been eclipsed by BookBub **www.BookBub.com**. BookBub now have five million subscribers. That's five million readers who download e-books. That's where your readers are; now you just have to be one of the books that BookBub accepts.

It's not easy to be one of the select few that these sites pick, and the submission requirements of each one vary. If you write erotica not every site will feature you; plus, no matter what genre your book is, you will need to have a minimum number of reviews and a minimum review rating in order to be considered. By this point that shouldn't be a problem; you should already have a number of reviews because of our pre-launch preparation.

Some of the stipulations that the promotional sites have are: how many reviews you have, your star rating, how long since you last ran a promotion, and the overall professionalism of your product (cover, synopsis, and presentation). I've put together a list of the current major sites to which you can submit your free book promotion, and they're included in the *Helpful Links* sheet at the back of the book. Some of these sites are free, and others will either charge you for a basic listing or have upgraded features that will guarantee you placement. BookBub, for example, is strictly a paid site.

All of these sites are Amazon affiliates. That means when someone purchases a book from them by clicking on the book's icon, the site is paid a small percentage of the sale. We discussed this earlier when we talked about Amazon's tools.

Early in 2013 Amazon modified the agreement it has with its affiliates. It now limits the number of free books affiliates can offer. If an affiliate doesn't abide by the rules, Amazon will drop them from the program, and the commission the affiliate was making on click-throughs will disappear. When this happened the sites had to scale back on the amount of free books they were offering, thus making it even more difficult to have your book featured. That's when the upgraded (for a fee) service came into play and sites that exclusively charge you (like BookBub) came to prominence.

The other option is to hire a firm to submit the details of your free promo to the top sites. I've used EBook Booster **ebookbooster.com/** several times. They currently charge $35 and will submit your promo to over 45 sites. I'd advise using them only if you'd prefer to spend that valuable time writing. If not, then you may as well save the money and submit to the sites yourself. In fact, on their main page they list the sites they submit to and give you links to reach them. You can use this as a guide to do your submissions. Or, Author Marketing Club has a page that lists quite a few of the major sites:

authormarketingclub.com/members/submit-your-book/

Sign up for their email newsletter to view the submission tool. Then you can click on the major sites directly. Author Marketing Club also has paid services that I have not utilized.

Additionally, there are always newer sites that will feature your book, and some of them might just become the next BookBub. I enjoy working with Kindle Books and Tips

www.fkbooksandtips.com/2013/07/03/6-free-discounted-kindle-books/

They have a very nice site that receives lots of traffic.

PeopleReads **www.peoplereads.com/** is another newer site that looks promising, as are The Fussy Librarian **www.thefussylibrarian.com/** and BookSends **booksends.com/**. Plus, Buck Books **buckbooks.net/** in a short period of time has become the number two ranked book promo site (according to alexa.com) after BookBub. They close to submissions from time to time but keep checking with them; it's worth it.

It's important to support the sites that you believe are going to work. You'll get a sense of this from the way the site is presented and in the manner that the administrators deal with you. It's easy to recognize professional behavior. If I believe in a site, I'll support it and tell others about it too.

When you see the list of sites in the *Helpful Links* section at the back of the book, it might feel as though you're going backwards to have to pay to promote a product that you're giving away, but supplementing your free promotion with a paid advertisement really has become necessary. When Amazon clamped down on its affiliates and limited the number of free books they could showcase, BookBub became a very important outlet. Currently, almost all of the books that have successful free runs are featured in a BookBub ad. The ads vary in pricing depending on which category your book is in, but you'll typically pay between $65 to $475 to promote the fact that you're giving your work away. Yep, I know it seems crazy, but in order to reach readers it is necessary.

Set a budget. If you can afford it, make sure BookBub is in your plans, and submit to as many sites as possible. Most are going to need a blurb, a picture of your cover, and confirmation that you have a set number of reviews and a certain average rating (4.0 is usually the norm). Later when we visit Chapter Eleven and discuss the Business of Writing we'll talk about media kits. This is a great example of where you can have your media kit open on your computer and copy and paste the information needed to the promotional sites. It'll save you time. And, if you find a more comprehensive list of promo sites than the one in the *Helpful Links* section, please let me know. I don't think there's one out there. This list is also included in the **Author's Tools tab** on my website, and I update it whenever I find a new outlet that might help spread the word about my book.

3. Social Network

When I ran my first few free promotions, I did some things that seemed worthwhile, but in hindsight I'm not so sure they were. For example, I ran ads on Craigslist. As most of you probably know, **www.craigslist.org** is a free website where everything and anything is sold and announced. I ran ads under the "Events" and "Books" sections announcing the dates and website of my free promotions. I took the time to run ads in major cities all over North America, and, as my book also takes place in the United Kingdom, I ran ads there too. The ads were free to run, but it wasn't really free because it took up my time, and my time could have been used in much more effective ways. I also spent a lot of time posting information about my book and my promotion on Facebook groups—a lot of Facebook groups. Some of them did help me find readers, but a lot of the groups were actually long threads of advertisements for books, and a lot of readers of those long threads were other authors. This is especially true now. If readers truly are reading those threads, then there are a lot of books for them to choose from. I tend to think that the majority of activity in most Facebook groups that are devoted to e-books is writers talking (and selling) to other writers. There's value in that too, but you need to draw the line somewhere and decide whether your time is best spent in that type of forum.

Having said that, social networks are still a very effective way of spreading the word about your free promotion. Typically, when you run a promotion for one of your books and have an ad running on a major site, the folks at the site will email you in the morning and give you the link showing where your book is featured. Eight a.m. is usually the time when your book will go live on the promo site. The site administrators will inform you that you'll see the main sales traffic occur once your book has been posted to the daily ad on their Facebook page. This is a fact, and I've seen it happen frequently. When I run ads, the majority of sales come once the site tweets the ad and posts it on Facebook. No matter what the critics (or cynics) say, when utilized correctly and respectfully, social networks are still incredibly powerful for getting the word out.

Although I believe the pages on some sites become too convoluted with advertisements, the above example shows that people continue to buy products when they're mentioned on Facebook, Twitter, and LinkedIn. We just have to remember to not take advantage of the relationships we've built. If you intend to run your book or books for free fairly consistently, you should be careful how often you inform your Facebook friends, Twitter followers, or LinkedIn contacts. If you're constantly letting them know that your book is free and asking them to share and retweet, your book will quickly gain a reputation as being the book that is always free. I've found it's more beneficial to post the link that shows the entire advertisement from the site you're featured on rather than just your book. This way you're sharing other books that are available, and your followers can check them out too. There are a lot of great books that are offered for free from time to time. If I find a book that I enjoy or believe in, I let my friends and followers know about it, and I've been thanked for referring books many times. People like free things, especially if it's something they're going to enjoy.

The same rules apply to any Yahoo Groups, KDP community forums, or Kboards that you participate in. Don't post your book too often, and if you're running free promotions consistently, post the whole ad, not just the link to your book. You will lose out on the affiliate revenue by doing this (by not posting your special affiliate link), but it's a far better tact to employ. And, you're much less likely to lose friends and followers.

Also, Facebook advertisements, as opposed to posts, can sometimes work to promote your free book. You've probably seen the pop-up notices in which Facebook prompts you to "promote your post," or Facebook has suggested that you try their paid advertising. I've tried this several times. It enables a lot more of your friends to see your post, raising it from that approximate seven percent mark we talked about earlier. Some authors have experienced an increase in sales (or free downloads) from running a Facebook ad. Mark Dawson has an excellent series of free videos **www.selfpublishingformula.com/** showing you how to utilize Facebook advertising to gain followers. The videos are full of useful information, and I suggest you view his tutorials before running your ad.

4. Time Your Run

The popularity charts are the categories that are toward the bottom of your product page. The popularity charts are where Amazon diverts readers when they're browsing for books. It's important to rank high on these charts. When I ran my free promotion I gave away fifty thousand books. Amazon credited those, on the popularity charts, as though I'd sold one-tenth of fifty thousand books. So, when my books became available at $3.99 again, I was at the top of the charts. Then when I sold thousands of books, I reached #4 overall among all of Amazon's paid books, and I stayed high in the rankings for quite some time. The month after, when Amazon tweaked its system, the payoff in terms of credits on the popularity charts lessened dramatically. As I mentioned, if I give away fifty thousand books today, the credit on the popularity charts is probably nil. This has made it much more difficult to get into the top ten.

The categories you picked when you initially uploaded your book are the same categories you'll be placed in when you run your free promo, but these will be listed in the free rankings. If your category is Romantic/Suspense, you'll be entered on that chart when you run your book for free too. You'll see it climb higher and higher in that category, and potentially you can reach #1 in the category or even #1 overall. This is a great accomplishment, and it's something you can use as a tagline in your promotions, but when one of my books reaches this peak, I don't consider that it's earned bestseller status—after all, nothing has been sold. I'm giving books away at this point.

The information I'm about to give you is very important. You have to end your free run on a high note. I ran a free promotion in June 2013 with *My Temporary Life*. Even though this book has been downloaded tens of thousands of times, free and paid, it's still a consistent seller for me, and every time I run a new promotion, I'm reaching all those readers who have purchased Kindles and iPads since the last time I promoted. There are always new customers for my book. I ran some paid advertising during the first day of my three-day promotion and it worked. During my first day I gave away twenty thousand e-books. I reached #4 overall on the free rankings charts too, so it was a very successful first day.

During the next two days (without the aid of paid ads), I only gave away an additional seven thousand e-books. This was still a lot but it certainly wasn't as strong as day one. I peaked early, and my book remained in the top twenty overall of the free rankings right up until the promo ended, but it wasn't good enough. When *My Temporary Life* returned as a paid product, the results were not good; in fact, they were very, very poor. I'd given away lots of books, hit the top ten and stayed there, yet my post-free results were only marginally better than what I'd been experiencing previous to the promotion. I covered the cost of my paid advertising (about $200 for Kindle Nation Daily and BookBub) and made a little more than that but not very much. It wasn't a disaster, though, because I learned something very valuable.

The following week, on the identical days that I ran my promotion, a colleague from my support group ran his promo, but we structured his differently. We timed his advertising (BookBub and Kindle Nation Daily), so that he was featured on those sites on his third day, and that's when he peaked. The difference was remarkable. He had twelve thousand free downloads and his book briefly hit #16 overall, but his post-free sales spike was ten times as strong as mine. Yes, ten times. He peaked at the correct time. It's important that you finish strong. We've tested this several times since then, and it seems to be very important to have your last day as your strongest day.

Now, you may suggest at this point that when your ranking begins to decline and your free downloads are tapering off, you should end your free promotion. You can do this; you can end it at any time by going to your KDP dashboard, halting your promo, and putting your price back to where it was beforehand. The problem with this is that you've probably made commitments to the sites that are featuring you and are advertising your promo. As I'm sure you've determined by now, you can't do this alone. You can advertise on your Facebook page, have friends tweeting details of your promo on Twitter, and post in every forum and social network known to man, but it's still not enough. Again, this has been tested, over and over again. We need help running these promotions. We need the assistance of the sites that have tens of thousands and in some cases, hundreds of thousands of subscribers. There aren't figures for every site but as I mentioned, BookBub have over five million subscribers on its email list. Their system is filtered so that they alert readers of a specific genre about a book that's free. As you can see, how and when you utilize sites like these is very, very important. If you've committed to running a promotion on certain days and they feature you on those days, your book should still be available for free.

The danger in not following the rules is getting that virtual asterisk beside your name, and the next time you submit your book for a promotion you may not make the cut. Yes, we're back to relationships and honoring the agreements we make with those who can help us the most. Don't pull out of a promotion too soon. Make sure you're not in contravention of any agreement you have with a site that is helping you out.

Another factor you have to take into account when timing your free run is how often you want to give your book away. There are authors whose books always seem to be part of a free promotion and others who space them out. I would recommend not running a giveaway any more frequently than once every six months. This is when having more than one book is a real advantage, especially if your books are part of a series, because you can rotate books and keep things fresh.

Unfortunately, the buying habits of consumers don't always make sense. When you have a series of books, you would think that giving away the first book would spur sales of the following books in the series. This isn't always the case. Sometimes it seems to be the second book or perhaps even the third that, when given away for free, spurs sales of the other books. Either way, my suggestion is to space out your free promotions. Take your time, let some new reviews come in, play with your product page, categories, keywords, and prepare for your next free run. And, most importantly, let Amazon sell some Kindle e-readers. Every time this happens you potentially have new customers.

Lastly, time your free run, if you can, to take place toward the end of the month. I've had a huge bonus when I've done this. I've received a lot—and I mean sometimes tens of thousands—of page reads through Kindle Unlimited when I go back as a paid sale at the beginning of a new month. Page reads or KENP are the other revenue stream that you'll receive by being in KDP Select. When readers are enrolled in Kindle Unlimited, they can read your book as part of their membership, and as an enrollee in KDP Select, your book qualifies. This can be a very nice source of revenue.

5.   Cross Your Fingers

I'm sorry, but it's true. I've seen some very good books do poorly when running a free promotion, and I've seen some poorly written work do very well. There are a lot of factors involved that you just can't control. I passed on running any types of promotions over Christmas 2012. I'd had a great year with my debut novel, I'd just released my second book, and I didn't want to compete with all the other authors who were trying to get a piece of that Christmas buying frenzy. In hindsight, I was wrong. Sales were very strong, and each of the following Christmases I was there, competing and trying to find readers.

As I said earlier, I've had some very successful free promotions and some that haven't worked out well. I know you're tired of hearing me say this, but the system has changed. Free promotions are not as consistently effective as they once were. Books in a series can succeed, and from time to time other books do very well, but the returns are not the same as they were five years ago. Fortunately, we have an alternative.

DISCOUNTED PROMOTIONS
1. **Pricing**
2. **Pick Your Days**
3. **Book Your Ads**
4. **Social Network**

5. **Cross Your Fingers**

1. **Pricing**

Free, as previously discussed, is not dead. Free promotions are fluky but sometimes do work. They help build your reader base for other books and will help increase the number of reviews you have. There is little downside. And, as mentioned, they may help you sell books. There are other ways to stimulate sales, and I'm going to break down the most foolproof way of running a discounted sale. We're going to talk about one of the other benefits of enrolling your book in KDP Select—Kindle Countdown Deals.

The idea behind the Countdown is similar to running a giveaway. We want to sell as many books as we can, albeit at the discounted price, and then when it returns to our regular pricing sell some at the higher price. The advantage to a Countdown deal is that your royalties paid will be 70% during the Countdown period as opposed to the 35% that is usually paid when your book sells below $2.99. The other advantage to a discounted promotion is that when your book gets closer to number one in the rankings, it registers on the "Paid" side of the chart as opposed to the "Free" side. This is important because once you go back to your retail price, your book will already be in position at a higher level than prior to the commencement of your promotion. One of two things will happen when your promotion concludes. After a few days your book will either fall back down the rankings and your sales will hit where they were previously or perhaps a little higher. Or, and I've seen this happen many times, your book will hit a relatively high level and maintain. The 10,000 to 12,000 overall ranking is a popular spot. Many authors, on releasing their books or running a promotion to freshen up sales, find that once they've spiked upward, their book will come back down and remain in that spot. This is a very good thing. If you reference the chart enclosed in the *Helpful Links* section, you'll see this equates to approximately ten to fifteen books a day. This is a good, constant revenue stream, and it allows you to continue writing and let your book sell on its own. Unfortunately, my books need a bit of help, and I have to run a new promotion monthly. I have six books, so it's easy to rotate them and offer a different deal each month. Hopefully your book will either shoot the lights out and stay in the top ten or at least find its spot and sell consistently.

There are a couple of ways to run your Countdown, but first I'll explain once again how it works. As part of your benefits under KDP Select you can run a Kindle Countdown deal for five days in every ninety-day period. During those five days you can discount your book either in one shot to $0.99 and leave it there for the period. Or, you can begin with $0.99 on day one and raise it back up to your retail price in increments. The preferred manner is a one-time drop. This almost always works and it's the method I use.

Ninety-nine cents seems to be a magic number and attracts eyeballs to your product page. If you've written a story that readers want to read, and it's presented in a professional manner, you will sell books at $0.99. But, it's not always necessary to reduce your price to $0.99. Sometimes a reduction from $4.99 to $2.99 is enough to generate sales. I discovered this during a Kindle Books and Tips promotion. I had just released the first edition of *How I Sold 30,000 eBooks on Amazon's Kindle-An Easy-To-Follow Self-Publishing Guidebook,* and it was selling very well. I'd booked the ad some time before I released the book, anticipating that it would need an initial boost. Fortunately that wasn't the case. My book got off to a very good start and was selling dozens of copies a day at $4.99. The promotion was one day long and I reduced my pricing to $0.99. It was successful. I sold several hundred books at that price level, and the next day, when I returned it to $4.99, more sales streamed in.

After a surge in sales it returned to its previous levels. I'd gone in with a strong book that was selling well at $4.99, and I should have reduced my pricing to $2.99. I may have had fewer sales, but the revenue would have been significantly higher. I was too quick to copy the methods of other authors. As you're no doubt aware by now, I keep an extremely close watch on what's working and what isn't, but it's important that we adapt those findings to our own situation. So, make the changes that help you. Our books will sell for whatever the market will bear, and sometimes that's a little bit more than what some other books are selling for. There's an old sales analogy that preaches, "Don't leave any money on the table." At $2.99, or even $4.99, my book was a great deal, and there was no reason to price it any lower. Lesson learned.

Due to the impact of KDP Select and the free promotion I ran, I sold thousands of copies of *My Temporary Life*. I was a very lucky guy. My book became an Amazon bestseller on the site's overall rankings and I received lots of media coverage, so quite a few people knew who I was. I was invited to write blogs for different websites, invited into online writers groups, and interviewed on radio shows. So the "cliff" that is talked about—that inevitable reckoning or evening of the playing field that happens when your book goes back to normal status and resumes sales at the level it was before your promotion—took a little longer to happen for me, but it did indeed happen.

With some exceptions, the "cliff" used to be thirty days. Thirty days after you'd run your promotion, your book would resume its previous sales levels. Today, you hit the "cliff" quicker, much quicker. In some instances it happens four to seven days afterward. Sometimes it'll stretch a little longer, but either way, it's probably going to happen. The happy authors who are the exceptions seem to find a ranking and stay there. Their books needed a little bit of visibility, and in running a promotion, they found readers and then hit a level of sales they were able to maintain.

The most notable difference I've found between free and discounted promotions is that when readers pay for your book, even if it's only $0.99, they'll actually read it. I don't believe that everyone who downloads a book for free reads it. Some do, because I've received some very nice emails and reviews from readers who have picked up my book for free, but for the most part I think a lot of those free downloads are still sitting on Kindles, unread. And when I, and you too, started this whole thing, the idea was to get readers to read our books. That's what I wanted, and I believe that if someone pays for a book, even if it's at a low price, they're more apt to read it.

Additionally, it just feels better. I'm an advocate of free promotions. They've been very, very good to me and my career, and I've written in glowing terms about them many times, and as outlined above, they can be effective, but when you're giving all those thousands of books away for free, it's sometimes hard to accept. We're giving away something that we've poured more than just work into for years, and really, we should be receiving some monetary value for it. So, when you're selling your book at a discounted price, at least you're receiving some royalties for your work.

My most recent novel was published by one of Amazon's imprints— Kindle Press. I'll talk more about how this happened toward the end of this book in the updated chapters, but while we're analyzing discounted pricing, I'll ask you to examine how Amazon's own publishing houses are currently discounting their books. Many of their promotions reduce the pricing to $1.99 as opposed to $0.99. My new book *The Dead List (A John Drake Mystery)* has been priced by Kindle Press at $2.99, and the first major promotion they ran was a price drop of a dollar to $1.99. There were thirty other books priced at the same level during the same promotion. All of the books were published by Amazon imprints. It was an extremely successful promotion even though the price drop was to $1.99 and not $0.99.

The challenge with a $1.99 ad as opposed to $0.99 is that it costs more to advertise on one of the promotion sites. The pricing level for the ad goes up if your book is on sale above $0.99. My spidey senses tell me that $1.99 is becoming a more effective price point to entice customers to check out your book. If I'm right, then hopefully author pressure will force the promo companies to reduce the pricing of ads promoting books at $1.99. And, I *hope* I'm right because a Countdown deal will earn the author an additional $0.70 per book sold. If Amazon with all of its marketing savvy is discounting to this level, then it's worth noting. And if $1.99 is truly the new $0.99 in terms of sale pricing effectiveness, then it's most definitely worth noting.

2. Pick Your Days

My current process is to run a Countdown sale for three, four, or five days, and as mentioned I employ a one-time drop to $0.99 or $1.99. The regular pricing of my books ranges from $2.99 for my shorter romance novella to $3.99 for my regular-length works of fiction, to $4.99 for the nonfiction work that you are currently reading (if you're reading the e-book version). I also have a book of short stories that always sells for either free or $0.99. This book would not qualify for a Countdown sale, as the regular price is too low.

The best days I've had for running a discounted promotion are on weekends. Saturdays and Sundays seem to be the busiest days. As we're going to discuss in a moment, it's imperative that you supplement your Countdown with a paid ad. This will limit the days available to you, and you may have to go with the day the site has open. If they allow you to pick—pick Saturday or Sunday.

Scheduling your paid ad in conjunction with your Countdown is very important. In the next section we'll discuss where to advertise, but in terms of timing we have to be aware of which day to run your ad. I like to begin my Countdown the day before my ad will run. This way I can be ensured that there are no errors on my side or Amazon's. Also, when you schedule your Countdown, you'll have the opportunity to pick which hour of the day you'd like to begin and end. Bear in mind all times are PST (West Coast of US and Canada). I like to begin mine at 5 a.m on Day One so I can hit both coasts at 8 a.m as people wake up, just in case someone has an overwhelming urge to purchase one of my books first thing in the morning. I run my paid ad on Day Two. I end my Countdown on the morning of Day Three. I've found that if I wait too long after the paid ad has run, the momentum may have lessened. So, it's important to get back to the regular retail price while your book is still strong in the rankings and selling. Here are some examples of typical recent Countdown timetables that have worked:

3-Day Countdown Sale
Day 1. Drop price to $0.99 or $1.99.
Day 2. Run a one-day ad to supplement Countdown; pricing remains at $0.99 or $1.99.
Day 3. Return pricing to regular level by no later than noon.

4-Day Countdown Sale

Day 1. Drop price to $0.99 or $1.99.

Day 2. Run a one-day ad to supplement Countdown; pricing remains at $0.99 or $1.99.

Day 3. Run an additional one-day ad to supplement Countdown; pricing remains at $0.99 or $1.99.

Day 4. Return pricing to regular level by no later than noon.

5-Day Countdown Sale

Day 1. Drop price to $0.99 or $1.99.

Day 2. Run a one-day ad to supplement Countdown; pricing remains at $0.99 or $1.99.

Day 3. Run an additional one-day ad to supplement Countdown; pricing remains at $0.99 or $1.99.

Day 4. Run an additional one-day ad to supplement Countdown; pricing remains at $0.99 or $1.99.

Day 5. Return pricing to regular level by no later than noon.

The "additional one-day ads" are on different sites from the original ad. This can be difficult to coordinate, as you may not always be able to book your preferred days. It is possible though. So, if you're able to run ads for two or even three days in a row—do it. Again, if possible, make sure your strongest promotional site is the one you use on the last day of your ads.

You may also want to experiment with different times. Some authors have success when the Countdown period ends at midnight or the early hours of the morning. In order to do this, end your promotion at midnight on the day your ad is running or the first few hours of the following day. If you leave it to midnight the day after your ad has run you may have fallen down the rankings too far and lost your momentum.

3. Book Your Ads

As you can see there's a bit of science to this. It's imperative that you supplement your Countdown sale with a paid ad. We're going to examine paid advertising. Here are three examples:

BookBub

https://www.BookBub.com/home/

If you're not tired of hearing about these guys by this point you will be soon. You'll hear them spoken of among your colleagues, in forums and groups, and of course on Facebook. They've built an extremely professional business and somehow managed to attract five million subscribers to their site. BookBub will give your sale traction. It's only been in a few isolated cases that I've heard of a BookBub ad being ineffective. The drawback of course is the cost. The cost for an ad promoting a discounted book is greater than an ad promoting a free book. Costs to promote a $0.99 book currently ranges from $80 to $620. The more popular and populous categories cost more of course.

A BookBub ad will help you sell books at the lower price, and your book will climb closer toward the top. And, if you've picked your categories as per our guidelines, you'll probably reach number one in your lesser-populated category. You're receiving a 70% royalty on $0.99, which is very generous, but your hard costs, the cost of the ad, has to be recovered. So it's important to get your book back to its retail pricing while the momentum continues.

Ereader News Today

ereadernewstoday.com/

ENT, as they're commonly and affectionately referred to, are still a very effective promotion site. In fact the return on investment can be far better than BookBub in some cases.

The only drawback to ENT's promotion is that typically they won't alert you that your book has been accepted until a few days before your requested date. At that time, immediately book your Countdown, and if you are utilizing any other smaller sites, request the dates to coincide with your ENT ad. Remember, you want to either run an ad on a smaller site on the same or preceding days of your major ad – Finish Strong!

Free Kindle Books and Tips

www.fkbooksandtips.com/

This is another progressive site that has built their subscriber base wisely. Although they don't have the numbers that some of the others do, I've always done well with their ads. They have different pricing levels that begin at $60. Almost all of the sites we talk about require that your book has a set number of reviews before it will be featured. FKBT has a unique offer where they'll promote your new release even if it has no reviews. This is mandatory for me when I release a new book. Pricing is reasonable and it gives you a nice initial boost.

The same rules apply for this and the other ads. Remember, timing is everything. Begin your promo the day before the ad kicks in, and then get out of there early the day after the ad expires.

Kindle Nation Daily

indie.kindlenationdaily.com/?page_id=642

This site is tougher for me to recommend. I've had some success with them, and other times it has not worked at all. During my workshops I demonstrate in-progress promotions. At one event we utilized Kindle Nation Daily or KND to feature my colleague's book for $0.99. We purchased their $99.99 sponsorship package and it did indeed work. Her book did very well. There have been other instances where KND has not worked. I find authors split on whether this site is effective. Tread carefully—$99.99 isn't cheap, but the results during our demonstration were quite impressive. Query your support group to determine the most current information on whether this site is working.

Buck Books

buckbooks.net/buck-books-promotions/

You know the horse that nobody wanted to wager on but you just have a feeling about it? You lay down your money while everyone else criticizes the pedigree, and lo and behold the horse comes in first—by a length and a half. These guys are the equivalent of that horse. They work on an affiliate system. They want you to sign up your friends so badly that they'll pay you a bounty when a few of them do so. In the process of building up all of this affiliate traffic, they put together an amazingly strong promotion site. Their ranking is number two to BookBub's number one according to Alexa. Their ad fees are reasonable, and I've had some very strong returns from their ads. Unfortunately the word is out and they close down submissions from time to time because they're swamped with promotion requests, but bookmark the site, and if you're able to place your book with them for a promotion—do it!

In writing this section I have branched out to as many forums and groups as I could. And of course I conferred with other authors. Although there are many, many sites that offer services, the above promotion sites are the closest thing to a guarantee.

There are others that are solidly building their subscriber base also:

The Fussy Librarian
www.thefussylibrarian.com/

PeopleReads
www.peoplereads.com/

Booktastic
booktastik.com/

Booksends
www.booksends.com/advertise.php

Some or all of them will grow to be part of our preferred list, and they need our support to get there. Their rates will remain low as they build, so don't forget about them. Perhaps supplement your major ad and spend a few dollars on one of the above or another site you believe in. Competition is healthy, and we need a selection of affordable sites where we can showcase our work. Also, in the *Helpful Links* list there are a number of sites that will feature your book when it is discounted, and they'll do this at no charge. If you take the time to submit to them, this can result in a few more sales.

4. Social Network

Yes, we're back here again. I will only promote my books during a sale on my preferred social networks as part of a whole package of books. So, if I have an ad on BookBub or ENT, I will post the link to the day's books that are on sale. I'll thank either BookBub or ENT for featuring me, and suggest to my friends and followers that they check out ALL of the books that are on sale. Then, I go and check them out myself and sometimes I purchase a book. I have a friend who confessed to me that she won't leave the house in the morning before checking out the day's offerings on BookBub and Buck Books. She does this every day and she sometimes purchases a couple of books. At two or three dollars per book it's a great deal. She's getting exposure to some great reads and they're always on sale. It's the only way she buys books, and she's thanked me for posting the links that first introduced her to the sites. Many other friends have expressed thanks also. If I'd been constantly promoting my own books or even my books along with my friend's books I would not have received the same reaction. I'm engaging with others and I post links to sites I believe in. I'm even making purchases myself.

Be careful of overexposing yourself by continuously promoting your own and your friends' work. Consider posting the whole link. The site-owners will be pleased and your followers will too. Social media can be amazingly simple. Hold up the mirror and decide whether you'd like to see the post you just typed into the little bar. Is it a message that will help you or will it make you wince and shake your head in frustration? As we spoke of earlier, there are indeed real people sitting at their computers. Treat them as such and you can't go wrong.

5. Cross Your Fingers

John le Carré, Nora Roberts, John Irving, Jude Deveraux, and Nevada Barr are some of the bestselling traditionally published authors who have featured their books at discounted prices on the sites I've referred you to. The sites that for the most part were built by self-published authors are now being utilized by traditional publishers to showcase their clients' books. The competition is fierce. It's an honor to see our books situated on the same pages as some of these fine author's books, but it also makes it tougher for unknown authors like me to stand out. This is where the need for professionalism is imperative. If you've followed our process, your book will not look out of place when advertised alongside the bestsellers, and after all, it's what we always wanted. We now have the same access to readers as the major players do. And, we're competing for the same discretionary dollars that they are.

Take pride that you've written a book that stands spine to virtual spine with these great authors' works. Oh, and hope that not too many of them decide to promote their books on the same day as yours. (And, cross your fingers too.)

The homework in this section could also be used as guidelines or general rules to follow when running your free or discounted promotion.

CHAPTER NINE HOMEWORK

1. If you have a minimum of ten reviews (in order to qualify for the promotion sites), book your first promotion. Make sure you *currently* have the minimum number of reviews because the promotional sites are going to look at your product page now, not on the day before your promotion. And give yourself enough time to get the word out.

2. When you schedule your ads, submit to every site that will accept your book. For this first run you should do it yourself; you can use EBookbooster some other time. For now you should familiarize yourself with all the sites and how they work.

3. Organize a social networking schedule and alert your followers on all your different sites. Schedule when and where you're going to announce, tweet, and email. You may want to organize a Facebook event for your first promotion. Begin sending invites about two

weeks previous to your sale. Don't worry about potential lost sales in the couple of weeks before your promotion; the bigger opportunity is just around the corner. And remember, post the link that shows all of the books that are on sale, not just yours.

4. Do a post-analysis once your promotion is over. Catalog how many books you gave away or sold at the discounted price, how many you sold afterward, and how long it took before your sales went back to where they were previously. Email the sites that featured you and thank them. If you're particularly impressed with coverage that you received, mention them in a blog and then send the link to the blog to the site administrators.

5. Plan your next promotion, but don't plan it too soon. Based on your analysis, what went right and what went wrong? What are you going to do differently next time? Was Twitter effective? Facebook? Was BookBub worth the money or has another site become popular?

CHAPTER EIGHT FOLLOW-UP

1. Are reviews continuing to come in? Are they being posted on Goodreads as well as Amazon's foreign sites? If not you need to submit to more reviewers.

2. Do you have some blogs written and ready to go? Always have some blogs in your back pocket just in case an opportunity comes up. Try writing about a current topic in the world of self-publishing, or why not list the best Indie books you've currently read, or the most and least effective ways you're finding of reaching readers. Or write about your recent promotion. Which site worked best in terms of getting the word out for you?

3. How's your product page looking? Does it need freshening up, or do you feel it's still effective?

4. Can you find one new way of reaching readers that you haven't read or heard about? How can you get the name of your book in front of someone today?

CHAPTER TEN
MORE PROMOTIONS
Or
How to Teach the World to Sing

I grew up in Scotland in the seventies, and I was exposed to some absolutely horrible popular music. Thankfully, punk rock came along and fixed all that, but for a period of time, when I was a young lad in short pants, wellington boots, and a balaclava, I had to listen to some real crap. One of the popular bands of the day was *The Seekers,* who later became *The New Seekers,* and yes, I'm not happy that I know these things. *The Seekers* was the first band that I was familiar with who sold out. They recorded a song that had become an anthem for Coca-Cola. "I'd Like to Buy the World a Coke" became "I'd Like to Teach the World to Sing." So Coke had a catchy song on their commercials, plus it became a hit and was played on radios all over the world. Even today, from time to time you'll hear someone humming or whistling the tune. I hate that song.

Coke loved it though. The exposure, to this day, is massive. You and I aren't going to get that type of exposure. I have an author friend who is plotting a rendezvous with an infamous movie star (you know, the busty one with the dark hair who's always pictured wearing a bikini). He feels that if he can have the paparazzi take a picture of him leaving a motel with said movie star, while one of them is holding a copy of his book (cover facing the camera of course), the exposure will help him reach every bestseller list known to man. I have another friend who is trying to orchestrate a story of his own demise and then miraculously come back to life just in time to greet the millions of readers who have bought his book while he was, um, not here.

None of these things are going to work, even if they were possible.

Even appearing on a nationally televised morning television show doesn't guarantee sales. Just ask Joe Konrath, the Indie pioneer who we spoke about earlier. Joe appeared on a nationally syndicated show and then sat back and waited for the sales spike to happen. It didn't. More people found out who Joe was. That's branding, and it's important too, but as new authors we want results and we want them quickly.

I rarely disagree with anyone online in forums and groups. I respect other people's opinions, offer my own and then usually move on, but one day that didn't happen. I was reading a thread in which a number of authors were despondent over their lack of sales, and an author who had several books out was talking about building your platform and waiting for readers to find your work. I agreed and disagreed. Yes, branding is important; people have to find out who you are and what you're about, but in the meantime all we want to do is sell a few books. The other author disagreed with me and talked about a slow steady rise (over some years presumably) where we'd eventually build a reader base and sell our books. I won't and don't do this. I want to sell books now, and everything I've talked about in this book is geared toward doing that.

The effectiveness of free promotions for me, and many others, has diminished. Some others still have some success with free promotions and use them as a main source for finding new readers. But ever since I ran my first KDP Select freebie, the post-free sales numbers have gone down. From time to time there is a slight increase but the effectiveness, for me, is declining. Because of this I've experimented with different ways to find readers. Some of these have been solo ventures, and some I've done with others.

One of my solo adventures took me on a walk around Vancouver International Airport. I handed out business cards to travelers who had Kindles or iPads in their hands. Fortunately, the security guards didn't see me. I also sent out press releases to newspapers telling them about my self-publishing success. I've written for major local newspapers on the subject of self-publishing, being mindful to include my book information in the article. And I've had book signings where I've sold my print books. From all of these things I have received other opportunities, and I met friends who have become some of my biggest supporters. All of these ventures were successful because they helped me find more readers, but I always felt that I was missing something.

For a while I kept having the same conversation with a fellow writer. We felt as though the concept or idea that was going to help us reach that next plateau of readership was right in front of us. We just couldn't see it. We could feel it; it was so close, but we couldn't figure out what it was. Well, there are two conclusions I've reached since we had those conversations. First of all, there are other methods of connecting with readers, and I'm going to show you how to effectively utilize them. The second conclusion I reached is that the other way to build your readership is to offer more content. Yes, it's hard to admit, but it might be the book. I may have written a book that doesn't appeal to the majority of readers. Maybe it's too early; maybe it'll be popular years from now. Or maybe I need to keep trying to become a better writer. I might have to go back to the very beginning and write another book. We should be doing this all along, of course, maintaining that balance and writing while we're promoting. But, before giving up on a work that has taken us months or years to complete, we need to exhaust all of the opportunities that are available to us. I'm going to break some of these opportunities down and show you what is currently working for me.

1. **Group Promotions/Box Sets**
2. **Traditional Outlets/Donations**
3. **Book Samples/Contests**
4. **Website/Newsletters**
5. **Book Signings/Speaking Events**

1. Group Promotions/Box Sets

I belong to a number of different online writers groups. There are lots of them to choose from, so when you do join a group choose wisely. My prerequisites are that I'm dealing with professional and progressive authors who work hard to expand their reader base. I'm happy to help new writers, and I often do, but in terms of advancing my career, I don't want to have to play catch-up with the others in my group. So I belong to a couple of groups, and we run group promotions. We're all independent business people, but running a promotion with a number of other authors, can really create some excitement. At the end of 2013 I ran a promotion with three other authors. Each of us writes in a different genre and each of us is fairly successful. We put together a box set of our e-books. We each included one book so that readers were exposed to all of our work. We offered the set for a limited time at a discounted price. Our price point for the set was $0.99, and we ran it during the Christmas season. Regular pricing was $4.00. Our hope was that after all those gifts had been opened and people were looking for e-books to load onto their new Kindles, they'd take a chance on our box set. It was a way for us to have access to each other's readers and followers, plus we were able to pool our marketing talents. Unfortunately, this venture did not work. I'm sure some of the sales on our other books were a result of our combined effort, but the set did not meet our expectations. In hindsight, I believe our genres were too mismatched to attract readers. Our set included a romance, a thriller, an adventure, and a coming of age story. For the most part readers stick with the genre that interests them. But, just because it didn't work for us, or we ran our promotion incorrectly, doesn't mean you should eliminate box sets. In fact, in the world of self-publishing, 2012 was called the year of the free e-books, 2013 was referred to as the year of discounted e-books, and 2014-15 were called the years of the box sets. Some authors have even reached the heights of *USA Today*'s bestseller list with their box sets.

These successful authors are either offering their own series of books in a set or they're combining with authors who write in the same genre. They discount their book for a limited period of time in order for it to hit those revered lists, and then they return it to the retail price. A box set that sells for four or five dollars and includes four or five books is a fantastic deal and readers are taking advantage of them. I have a friend who is a well-known romance author. The sales on her other books rose by 50% when she participated in a box set with four other authors, and maintained at that level for months. It's working. There are some significant success stories happening every day due to box sets. If you have a completed series or are invited to participate in a team effort with other authors, jump at it. Make sure the others are running their careers in the same manner as you are and that they have readers for their books. Go ahead and take a chance.

I've also participated in other group promotions. At the beginning of 2016 the folks at Buck Books (also called Goodriter) included the 2015 version of the book you're reading in a group promotion. Again, there were a number of authors, of similar genres (writing and publishing guides), and our books were priced lower for a limited period of time. This was not a boxed set type of endeavor. Readers were directed to a central web page that showed all of our books and then had a click-through that directed them to Amazon for the lower price.

The folks at Buck Books/Goodriter have some seriously positive mojo happening. We blew the doors off of Amazon and took over several categories. This promotion was extremely successful, and my book did very well. Their ad was simple yet professional, and they managed to rally authors and readers to yell about the promotion from the rooftops.

If you're facilitating a group promotion by yourself, pick the days to run your deal, drop your pricing, assign each member different tasks, buy some advertising (if you approach some of the sites and let them know what you're doing they may offer you a discount), and then get the word out there. I've seen group promotions where the subsequent sales for certain authors' books within the group have never been the same. It's helped the authors to cross boundaries and find readers, and they've never looked back. Amazon's major promotions spotlight the company's top one hundred authors, or top-rated authors. The promotions I participated in were another way to showcase quality books as part of a group enterprise. I believe it's the next step that can help us reach the next tier, and of course it ties in with my personal philosophy of helping each other.

When you organize your group promotions, it's very important to choose the correct participants. Make sure the others in the group have a product that you're proud to have sitting beside yours in an advertisement. Make sure they're willing to put the work into making the promotion a success. And make sure they're selling books, or they've at least sold books in the past. In running these types of efforts, you're not just going to find readers who've never heard of you or your books, but you could also be exposed to new forums and promotional sites that may be helpful to you in the future. This is where supplementing your ads by social networking is even easier, because you're going to expose your friends and their friends not only to your work but also to the work of the others in your group.

There really is nothing to lose with this type of venture. Again, the most effective price point seems to be $0.99 or $1.99, but the discount from $4.99 to $2.99 will work from time to time in a group promotion, so experiment with both as long as there's consistency within the group and everyone is offering the same discount.

2. Traditional Outlets/Donations

As we mentioned when we planned your book launch, traditional outlets can help us spread the word. Even though we voluntarily quarantine ourselves and sit in front of a computer for hours each day, creating wonderful work and comparing notes with our colleagues, there are still folks who read newspapers and magazines, and some even watch television.

When I hit a cliff in mid-2012 and my book found its natural sales rhythm of selling five to ten books a day, I started to look for other ways to get the word out. I had other promotions planned, of course, but in between that time I wanted to keep talking about myself and my books, so I wrote some newspaper articles. I wrote an article about where to find readers for e-books, and I wrote another about giving books away. I had no idea what I was going to do with them, but I wrote them and then submitted them to several newspapers. One of the newspapers published the articles, and, like so many other things that happened, other opportunities appeared because of the articles. I was approached by an audio company that offered me a contract to make audio versions of my books; I was hired by a writing school to teach workshops helping authors to self-publish, and I was invited to speak at writers groups and conferences. Everything leads to something else, and you never know who might be reading your work or watching your career.

As your name and books become better known, you'll be asked to give a little bit here and there too. I've donated books to libraries that were ravaged by a hurricane, and I've donated books to other causes that I wanted to support. These are print books, of course, and the most effective way to send books (if you've followed our system and published through CreateSpace), is to send your books directly from CreateSpace to the recipient. This will cut down on your cost of shipping. Once you've made your donation, you may want to consider letting your local newspaper know. It's easy enough to send a quick email to your paper and tell them how you're helping out. I've done this several times and received some very nice press because of it. And don't be concerned if it's a small newspaper that interviews you. If the story is newsworthy enough, other papers might pick it up, and your coverage will increase substantially.

3. Book Samples/Contests

After releasing my second novel at the beginning of 2013, I had a feeling that I wasn't going to be able to produce the next book in the series for some time. You know how sometimes you just—know. Well, I knew. I also knew that I had to get something in front of the readers who had so kindly supported me. I wanted to keep my name and books current, so I put together a collection of short stories. I had three or four stories that I'd worked on over the years; I freshened those up and included them. I had another that I'd written for an online magazine. After obtaining permission from them (in return for including a link to their site), I included it too. And, I included the first chapters of each of my novels. Each chapter one was written in such a way that it could be considered a short story, so they were a good fit. I inserted the link to the buy page/Amazon product page at the end of each of the chapters and suggested that if the reader would like more they could take a peek. At the end of the book I included my media kit that gave my bio as well as sample reviews and the buy links to all of my work.

I had no intention of making money from this venture, so I priced it at $0.99 and from time to time I give it away. I had the work professionally edited, and my cover designer came up with a fantastic cover. In April

2013 *Lies I Never Told – A Collection of Short Stories* was born. It gave me an opportunity to keep in touch with my readers and tell them I had a new book out that they might want to consider. This project worked very well, and I don't know why other authors don't follow suit. I sell several copies of the collection each month, and when I give it away the numbers are in the high hundreds. This is a book I enjoy giving away. I'm proud of the work, and I feel that if readers like it, they may purchase my other books. In time I may even release a newer version, or I might add some stories to the existing book. Every time I give a copy away or sell one it makes me smile. It's a terrific way to introduce readers to my fiction, and as an added bonus the collection has been reviewed very well. Readers have enjoyed the stories.

Consider releasing a book of stories and include the first chapter or chapters of your already published work. Make sure you're proud of the content. Don't release old high-school stories that you think readers will be interested in (unless they're of sterling quality). No one wants to see our progression as writers. Even mega-selling authors have trouble selling their early works. If I (and your other readers) purchase a book, we want it to be worthy of our reading time. Although I'm a fan and follow several authors, I'm not interested in reading their less-polished prose. Make sure the work is top-notch, go through the same editing, cover design, and formatting processes that we've outlined, and release your book. It's an ongoing way of reaching new readers.

I was approached by a website and asked to give away an e-book copy of my debut novel as a prize in a contest shortly after I'd published. The sites' subscribers primarily read romance novels. Even though it is not a traditional romance, they felt my book would appeal to their readers. I committed ten e-books to their contest, and it was one of the best decisions I've made. From those ten winners I've gained followers who have reviewed and spread the word about my book far and wide. Three of those initial winners have become fervent supporters of my work. They've told me if they hadn't won my book they would never have checked it out.

I believe that if we win a prize in a contest it represents something of value to us. Even if it's an item that we normally would not invest in, it still has some value because it was a prize in a contest. Those folks who won my book read it. If they'd seen it on Amazon's pages they would have kept clicking on to the next image, but it had some value so they checked it out. Fortunately, most of them really liked my book. Several of them contacted me afterward to thank me and offered to spread the word. They also wanted to know if I had any other books, and asked me to contact them once I had released more. Give your books away as prizes. It'll expose you to readers who may not normally look at your book. We all believe in our work. We feel that if we can reach readers, even those who regularly read in other genres, they might just fall in love with our book. Participate in contests; it's a great way to reach a whole new section of readers.

4. Website/Newsletters

I made an adjustment at the beginning of 2014. I'd purchased my domain name—**martincrosbie.com**—early in my career, and I'd put together a very basic website. I posted my blogs on my site and from time to time updated my coming events. I didn't have time to keep my website fresh, and instead I diverted interested readers to my Amazon Author Central page. As you know, your Author Central page contains upcoming events, your Twitter feed, and links to your blogs. At the time it was the right decision because it kept my maintenance down and allowed me to keep writing. As my career expanded though, and I began teaching and speaking at more workshops and events, I decided I wanted my own space. With the help of a creative web design person, we totally redesigned my website. Today I have a professional, accessible area where readers, and other authors, can find out what I'm up to.

Your website should always be a work in progress. You should constantly be on the lookout for new and creative ways to engage the viewers. I installed Google Analytics on my site to help me analyze who visits me. This measures the number of visitors, how long they stay, where they're from, and many other valuable pieces of information. I'm now familiar with terms like "bounce rate" and "unique visitors," and I look for ways to make my site more accessible to the readers and followers I send there.

At the end of every self-publishing instruction presentation I give, I always end with a slide or handout that says "What Can I Do For You?" Then I list different ways I can help the author. I do this on my website too. I have a tab that gives away all kinds of valuable information. It includes some of the things you're receiving in this book—places to procure photos and images for free, review sites, promotion sites, and more. By giving away this information in a designated tab, my hope is that viewers will spend a bit of time there and find out more about me. And my books are advertised on my site too, of course. If you're speaking in person at an event, try to collect email addresses and send out the most updated information you have after the fact, rather than distribute handouts. This enables you to build your contact list. My primary purpose is to find readers for my books. I never forget that.

As you speak at different events, interact with readers who comment on your blogs, or even when you receive correspondence from folks who have enjoyed your books, you will accumulate contact information—yes, email addresses. These should be kept in a contact list. Different areas have different laws regarding privacy issues when it comes to procuring email addresses. Most of them rely on the basic premise that you have to ask permission before emailing someone. If a follower clicks on your "follow me" or "subscribe to my newsletter" button on your website, then you have permission to converse with them, of course. At speaking events, make sure you hand out a form asking whether the person would like to be contacted about upcoming events or work. Familiarize yourself with your local laws and restrictions before adding an email address to your list of contacts.

5. Book Signings/Speaking Events

Book signings are another great way to get your name and book in front of readers. One of the incorrect statements that I hear from time to time is that self-published authors can't sell their books in brick and mortar bookstores. Or that we have to hire outside firms and have them distribute our books to stores. In fact I've attended writers festivals where traditional publishers spout this same fallacy. This is incorrect. I'll say it again—this statement is most definitely incorrect. Bookstores will accept self-published books.

If you've released your print book through CreateSpace, you're eligible for the (now free) Expanded Distribution feature. This will help you get your book into stores. All you have to do is knock on some doors. Bookstores want books that sell. I approached a local store (which has several outlets), told them I'd given away fifty thousand e-books and asked if they'd be interested in selling my print books. They ordered some and the books sold, and they continue to carry my books. From there I posted a picture on Facebook of my book on their shelf, and a friend of a friend who manages a supermarket decided that if my book was on a physical shelf (as opposed to a virtual one), he'd order some books too. That got me into a chain of supermarkets.

Once my book began selling, one of the branches of the independent bookstores invited me to spend a Sunday afternoon signing books. They advertised the signing on their store's website and posted notices all over the neighborhood. I held a Facebook event and invited local friends and posted details on my website. On the day of the event my significant other stood at the entrance to the store with a plate of warm, homemade chocolate chip cookies, inviting folks to come in. We had quite a crowd. Weeks afterward, staff members from the store were still talking about how successful the event was. Oh, and the store sold a number of books that afternoon, some of which I had written and some I had not.

Some of this was luck, but it was self-made luck. I kept looking for ways to get my book out there and I found them. You'll discover other opportunities too. I've sold print books at garage sales, craft sales, just about anywhere that I can get in front of people who might want to read my work. The interesting thing I've found is that although this has helped me sell print books, and that in itself is a fantastic thing, some readers love their Kindles, and if they see the print book they might just buy the e-book, instead of or in addition to the print version. This has happened to me time and time again.

Don't discount opportunities. Knock on some doors of bookstores and ask. Today my book, the same self-published book that I was told could not be sold in bookstores, is available all over the world including Powell's, the world's biggest bookstore. So, go ahead, tell me it can't be done. I dare you.

Some days I believe I'm running the Wizard from the Wizard of Oz strategy. I feel like I've created enough smoke and mirrors to dupe the occasional passerby into thinking that I'm a much bigger deal than I really am (by accentuating my positive accomplishments). Then other days when mention.net sends me alerts that tell me my name is being bandied about in fairly exclusive circles, I begin to believe once again that I have accomplished a thing or two. In order to forward your career to the next level, you need to believe a little bit of both of these things. You need to retain your humility because if you don't, it shows—online and in real life. But you also have to sell yourself and your accomplishments too. If you adhere to the pay it forward philosophy that we've talked about, and when accepting accolades recognize that your accomplishments were made possible because of the help of your peers, you'll be able to showcase yourself and keep your feet planted on the ground.

I began teaching self-publishing workshops in the fall of 2013. In order to fill seats at my weekend events, I needed to branch out and find writers who might be interested in attending my classes. I visited writers groups and other writing events. The challenge wasn't finding events and groups: there are lots of them. The challenge is convincing the group facilitators that you have something to offer their members. This is when you need to find a way to illustrate your accomplishments. I had a message to offer. My mandate is to try to help raise the professionalism of self-published books. In submitting a request to speak to a group or at an event, I outlined my philosophy and told the group what I could do for them.

I've spoken at groups and events where there were only a handful of authors present, and I've given talks at events where the room was overflowing. In addition to signing up interested authors for my workshops, I've also sold print books, and I've sometimes seen e-book sales surge afterward. And, more importantly, each time I've given a talk a new opportunity has arisen. A talk at a writers group has led to a presentation at a local library. A library has led to a mini-workshop offering and it goes on and on. Start with a small event. Practice your talk beforehand, and when you attend enjoy the fact that you're in a room with all those creative minds. Speaking events will separate you from the crowd. Approach the group with the intention of doing something for them. It will always pay off, and you'll be surprised at the opportunities that may be presented to you.

Staying ahead of the curve is important, but this is easier said than done. As I've said, I keep my ear to the ground, and I like to think I know what's happening out there. Part of the information comes organically because I've surrounded myself with strong colleagues, and I'm lucky enough that they share their findings with me. And, part of it is just a natural hunger to know what's working and how it's working.

One of the things I admire about Amazon is that it never sits still. It's always changing and either anticipating market changes or even forcing market changes. In my own little way, I try to do the same. If my sales are stalled for a few days, I search out new keywords and make the changes. Or I switch categories for a week or two to see if I can find some new readers. Neither of these things costs any money and the switchover takes only a few hours, so why wouldn't I try? I might find that magic place where my book should be. The secret isn't just finding the information; it's using what you've learned.

At the outset I told you I was going to help you produce your book in the most professional and efficient manner possible. I can give you the information, and I've tried to do that, but you have to use it. During my workshops I attempt to cram as much information into a weekend as possible and help as many authors as I can. My partner in this venture is an experienced instructor, and the statistics she gives me aren't encouraging. She tells me that less than ten percent of folks who attend workshops or read books put the information into practice. I want to change that. I hope that you take the systems I've shared with you, the same systems the top five percent of successful authors are utilizing, and use them to sell your books. The secret to all of this, if there is indeed a secret, is to do the work.

If you do the work and continue to subscribe to the—yep, here it comes again—pay it forward philosophy, you will indeed stay ahead of the curve.

CHAPTER TEN HOMEWORK

1. Organize and plan a group promotion. Ideally you should have different group members for each venture so that you're finding new readers each time.
2. Submit an article to several print periodicals. Include your bio and, if necessary, utilize the Wizard of Oz strategy (accentuate your fantastic accomplishments).
3. Query local book and writer groups and events and offer to give a talk on your self-publishing experience.
4. Find one new way to get your name and book in front of readers. Just one—
   that's all it takes.

CHAPTER NINE FOLLOW-UP

1. Have you assessed your free promotion and charted your next course? Make sure you're comfortable with your plan for your next free promotion.
2. Are you following up on all your emails in a timely manner? By this point you'll be receiving emails from readers; when you reply to thank them, make sure you ask how they heard about your book. This is vital information, and marketing companies pay lots of money to discover the answer to that question. You have the answer right at your fingertips.

CHAPTER ELEVEN
THE BUSINESS OF WRITING

By this point your thinking has changed, or perhaps you thought of yourself as a business person all along. Either way, you now understand that in order to be successful you either have to write a book that takes off on its own like the Hugh Howey example cited earlier, or you need to work to get the word out, as I do with my books. We spoke about balance, and in the next chapter I'm going to show you how to maintain your balance and make writing your priority. We've also worked on your product presentation, and we've discussed the most effective forms of marketing. There are also some other tasks I do to organize my business. Don't worry; these aren't major time-drains. These are things that are going to help you devote more time to writing.

1. Destroying the Pirates
2. Creating a Media Kit
3. Scheduling
4. Creating and Maintaining Your Website
5. Farming Out Tasks

1. Destroying the Pirates

We spoke about piracy sites earlier. These are sites where someone has a copy of your book and gives it away for free. This happened to me within the first couple of months of publishing my debut novel. I'm going to show you how to find, recognize and destroy—I mean subdue—I mean have the piracy site remove your book.

There are piracy sites and malware sites. Both will purport to have copies of your book available for free download. If you've set up your

Mention.com or Google Alerts accounts to notify you when your book title is being used, they'll send you a message when your book pops up on a website. Sometimes it's a review or an interview, but unfortunately it can be a piracy site too. If it is indeed a piracy site, there will usually be a section where you can send the site owner a Digital Millennium Copyright Act, or DMCA, takedown notice. If there isn't a section, then locate the contact email address for the site and send them a DMCA notice. I've included a template for a DMCA in the *Helpful Links* section. You're welcome!

When I've sent out a DMCA to a pirate site that is advertising my book, it's always been removed. I've been lucky. Sometimes it can take a while, and sometimes you have to contact them a number of times.

The other alert you'll receive will be for a site that claims to have your book available for free download, but in fact the intention is to send a virus to the user's computer. You'll recognize these malware sites when you examine them more closely and see that a credit card or other personal information is required before you can progress to the download stage. Leave these strange people alone. Karma will come and bite them in the rear.

2. Creating a Media Kit

Assume that you're going to hit it big. Once you've published your book, things might just go nuts. It's happened before. And, if it does go crazy, or, even if it doesn't, you're still going to need to tell the world a bit about yourself. Whether you're submitting your information to a blogger who has invited you to write a guest blog, to an interviewer who wants to talk to you on a podcast, or if Jeff Bezos (Mr. Amazon himself), calls to tell you that he was up all night reading your book and wants to feature you on Amazon's home page—you'll need a media kit. They tend to come in handy.

I keep an ongoing media kit updated at all times. It began as several pages, but as I've written more books and spread my virtual wings wider, the size of the kit has increased. The first section has my picture and bio (copied directly from Amazon). Below that I have all my contact information—Twitter, Facebook, my website address, my email address, and the link to my Amazon Author Central page. The next section has links to a couple of selected articles that have been written about me, and links to a couple of articles that I've written. For example, I have the main articles that were written about my self-publishing journey as well as links to articles that I've written for Indies Unlimited and other sites. Then I have a section for my books. For each book, I include the cover, a synopsis, links to the purchase page, and a couple of reviews. The buy links of course are my own personal links through the Amazon Associate program (as mentioned in Chapter Seven), so I can earn additional revenue when my books are sold. I include the buy links for Amazon.com, .co.uk, and .ca. At the end of the media kit, I list ways to connect with me, and include my contact information once again. This lets me list my information twice, and my potential interviewer or reviewer doesn't have to scroll back to the top.

When submitting, some sites will have forms that require you to fill out specific information; for others you can just send your media kit. When creating your kit, keep the tone friendly, yet professional, and make it simple for the user to navigate. The intention is to save busy bloggers or radio hosts some time. Hopefully, they will read your press kit, be impressed by your accomplishments and how professionally your information was provided, and invite you to write for their website, appear on their radio show, or have lunch with them (if it's Mr. Bezos).

If I find a blog site that I like and think I may have an article I'd like to contribute to them, or if I contact a library or writers festival and ask if perhaps I might be able to participate in one of their events, they need to know who I am. This is where I use my media kit. I send them a brief email and tell them a bit about my work and myself and include my media kit. Or, when I'm submitting to promotion sites, it's far easier to have the file that includes my media kit open on my computer and copy and paste the information that they need. It saves a lot of time. This goes back to finding more time to write instead of having to deal with the business end.

I have an abbreviated version of my media kit inserted as part of the back matter of my books. It's misleading to readers if you make this section too long because they're expecting content. Include brief mentions of your other publications (very short synopsis, buy link, and one catchy sentence from a review), your contact information, and a very short bio. If you make it too long, readers won't appreciate it. Keep it just wordy enough to be interesting.

Put together a regular and abbreviated media kit. I guarantee you'll utilize them and it will help save you time.

3. Scheduling

I'm a lists guy. I love lists. I love adding things to my list and then crossing them off. Sometimes I'll add an item that I've already completed just so I can cross it off. I use three very basic lists in organizing my day to day and beyond projects—a "Things to Do" list, a daily word count spreadsheet, and an upcoming promotion scheduler. I'll break down each one for you.

I use an old-fashioned "Things to Do" list. I keep it on the desktop of my computer and in my documents folder. The items are not prioritized; I know they all need to be completed, and if there is a line that remains there longer than it should, I always get it tackled. Currently I'm working on three different books—all three have their own line on my list. The reminder to do revisions for the book you are reading is on one line. I have a line reminding me that I have an article I need to complete; I have a list of items I want my web-person to address (I'll explain more about this fabulous person in point #5); and I have a number of folks who'd like print copies of my books—they are on their own lines too. As I complete each task, I put a line through it with that great little tool Microsoft Word offers, and then it's done. I leave the completed task on there for a few days so I remember that it has indeed been handled.

My "daily word count" is on an Excel spreadsheet. In the next chapter I'll explain how to get in the habit of writing every day. This is the sheet where I record my word count. The headings list the date, the day number (since inception), the project I worked on, and the amount of words written. It's a great way to keep track of which projects I'm favoring. And on the days when I feel as though I'm not getting anywhere, I can refer to it and see how much writing I'm actually accomplishing.

My scheduler is also on an Excel spreadsheet. I currently have six books available for sale and all doing well. I'll have seven by the end of the year. When I only had one book, I'd run a promotion on it once every three months, and I'd blog and request interviews in between that time. Now I'm spoiled. I can run a promotion on a different book each month. This is a great advantage. The only challenge is trying to remember where and when I've promoted each book. That's where my scheduler comes in handy. I record where I'm going to promote each book three months in advance. Most, if not all, promotion sites don't want to hear from you three months before your desired promotion date. So, your scheduler is also a wish-list. I pick out a book, where I want to promote it, and what I'm going to do with it. For example, if I want to run an ad on BookBub in conjunction with a Kindle Countdown Deal and put my book on sale at $0.99, I'll enter it in my scheduler. I'll do this for each of the upcoming three months.

The challenge is that BookBub may not accept my book. Then I need to go with my backup plan. I stick with the same book, as I don't want to overexpose my most popular book, and I submit it to a different site. Invariably, another site will agree to the promotion. In my scheduler I record that BookBub did not accept my book, and I note where I ended up promoting it, and what I did with it (Kindle Countdown, giveaway etc.). The sales numbers from the promotion are included in my KDP dashboard, so there's no need for me to record those.

So, with the scheduler I can quickly see what and where I've promoted, check out my KDP dashboard and determine whether the promotion worked, and decide what I'm going to do next. I urge you to use a scheduler, especially if you have multiple books or plan on publishing multiple books. It will eliminate any chance of overexposing one book, and you'll know what's working and what isn't.

4. Creating and Maintaining Your Website

I've included this section toward the end of this book because you have much more important tasks to address before working on your website. Author Central is a good, temporary substitute. At some point, though, you will need a destination where you can send your readers and followers. My website includes tabs for upcoming events, my blog posts, information on my books, a bio, a latest news section, and of course a tab that has my contact information. I've also added two other tabs recently.

One of the really nice by-products of having self-published my books and experiencing a little bit of success has been the opportunity to speak at different events. After teaching a workshop in the fall of 2013, I realized how much I enjoyed trying to get my message of producing professional self-published product out to authors. So, I decided I wanted to do more of it. I now have a speaking/blogging tab on my website. It includes brief testimonials from folks who have invited me to speak at their events or write for their blogs as well as a statement from me letting everyone know that I am available to speak or write articles. This is a great area to direct folks to when I'm interested in being invited to a festival or writing for a publication.

Additionally, I have a tab titled *Author's Tools*. This is the high-traffic area of my site. Under the tab I've included promotion sites, editor, formatter, and cover designer contact info, places where you can access free images and photos, lists of review sites where you can submit your books, and some Twitter hashtags that are helpful in promoting your book. It's a great way to get traffic to my site, and I believe it helps with my bounce rate. Don't I sound important when I use tech-speak? Your bounce rate, as many of you know, measures the percentage of users who leave after viewing only the entrance page and not pursuing other pages. We want readers to come to our site and look around. Spreading useful information on different pages helps get readers to stick around.

As I mentioned earlier, in order to gauge the effectiveness of my site, I installed the Google Analytics plug-in. This will measure not only your bounce rate but also the number of visitors and where they're coming from. Remember, your website will always and should always be a work in progress. If your career changes to include other facets (speaking, teaching) you will revise your pages. And, as you create new ways to interact and draw users to your site, you'll make changes. Having an easy to follow, functioning website is the next step in your professionalism as an author. And building your email list is mandatory as your career progresses.

Amazon have the contact information of your readers but you do not. It's in your best interest to continue building that list. Having a professional website is most definitely an important component of the business of writing. As my career became busier and I needed to tip the scales toward more writing and less business-type tasks, I realized I needed help in some areas. Website design and upkeep was one of those time-draining areas toward which I did not want to devote my valuable energies. In the next section I'll show you how I overcame this challenge.

5. Farming Out Tasks

Much of my income is derived from writing books. I need to write and create and produce material. If I'm not doing this, my readers will purchase books elsewhere. In the next chapter I'm going to show you how to put more time into writing as opposed to marketing, but before we get there I'm going to show you another way to save time.

I'm fairly tech-savvy. I know my way around a computer and the Internet, and if I come across a task that I can't figure out, I'll sit for hours until I teach myself how to do it. I've done this many times, and I've come to the realization that it's not worth it. Again, I have readers who are waiting for my next book. I'm a very lucky guy. So, I should be writing. That's why I got some help.

As you know, we need to hire a professional to format, edit, and cover design our work. I also hired a web designer to freshen up my website, and I employ her to deal with the tech-type tasks that I either don't know how to do or shouldn't be devoting my time to doing. For example, I have a very nice banner on my Facebook and Twitter pages. It shows a picture of me as well as my books laid out in a row. I've had a lot of compliments on it. My web person put that together for me. She did a far better job than I would have and did in minutes what would have taken me at least a whole evening. If I have a minor irritation on my website and can't figure out how to correct it, or if I want some help designing a newsletter, or any of the other tasks that would take her minutes—as opposed to the hours that I might put in—I ask for help. Fortunately, this does not have to be a costly expense.

I budget out how much to spend on outside help from my tech person, and I adhere to that number each month. If you can only afford $25 or $50 and you feel that it will help free you up to get back to writing then spend the money. Use the same justification that I employ. If it's something that takes a professional minutes to complete and will take me hours, then I'll pay to have it done. My monthly budget is less than $100, and that's helped add many hours of writing time to my schedule. Consider hiring a professional; it might just make the difference between having time to complete your book or having it languish on your computer while you deal with techy tasks. At the risk of having my valuable helper overrun with outside work, I have included her contact information in the *Helpful Links* section. Your other alternative is to again confer with your support group and find out whom the top performers are using to assist them.

In less than five years, I feel as though I've gone from flailing around in the water and occasionally swimming forward to moving forward with almost every move I make. I've become far better organized than I was at the beginning, and the organization that consists of the simple tools and systems listed above continues to improve. When you examine the above tasks, you may feel that it's more work, and it is, but in one evening you will be able to complete the groundwork required to get these tasks started. Put the work into developing systems. If the above doesn't work, then come up with your own. Make sure you know where you've been, where you're going, and how you're going to get there.

CHAPTER ELEVEN HOMEWORK

1. Create a couple of media kits—one longer and detailed and a more concise version. Make sure you include all your relevant information and that your links are live.
2. Set up and organize schedules for daily writing; daily, weekly, and monthly tasks; and a schedule of where you'll be running your promotions. Bear in mind this will be partly a wish-list determined

by which sites accept your submission.

3. Plan out how you'd like to organize your website and begin interviewing tech-persons who may be able to assist you. Query your support group, and you'll probably find a suitable candidate.

4. Set a budget for hiring outside help and adhere to your budget.

CHAPTER TEN FOLLOW-UP

1. Have you organized and executed a group promotion yet? Analyze the results.

2. Do you have enough books published that you can incorporate them in a box set? Make a wish list of authors you'd like to produce a box set with. You never know—maybe they'll say yes if you approach them. Visualization works!

3. How's your speaking career progressing? Have you queried local writers groups yet? Start with a small group and practice speaking and reading from your work.

CHAPTER TWELVE
FINDING A BALANCE

If you fly by the seat of your pants and try everything all the time, you'll drive yourself crazy. You might experience some success from time to time, in fact I'm sure you will, but you'll also drive yourself nuts. You need a plan. We all do. You need to plan when you're going to run free promotions, and you need to plan when you're going to run discounted promotions. You need to have some newspaper articles and blogs either in the works or stored on your computer, ready to submit. And you need to take the time to approach bookstores and organize book signings. And, most importantly, you need to write another book. Yep, we're back at that again.

Earlier, much earlier, we talked about balance and how important it is to keep working on content. We haven't revisited it much since earlier in the book, but it's still extremely important. Once you've tackled all the tasks I've given you, a system will fall into place. You'll know how and where to submit your work, you'll develop a name and reputation, and you'll develop relationships with people who can help you. Opportunities will begin to come to you. This will happen because you organized and made a plan for your writing career.

When you began writing, you planned on writing a book, and when you finished you planned on publishing your book, and then, when you picked up this book, you were using it as a tool because you planned on finding readers for your book. Now you have to break down that part of the plan and be more specific about where you're going to apply your efforts.

Plan your time wisely and remember—you need more material, and if I can do it, you can too. I'm not special, but I do work hard. I still work part-time at my previous occupation. I still run, spend time with friends and family, and I even goof off once in a while, and because I follow the systems outlined in this book I've produced more content too. That's because I plan what I'm going to do and when I'm going to do it. To get consistent results you need to make a plan. I'd be lost without mine.

The one question I'm asked over and over again when I facilitate workshops or speak to writers groups is: How do you find the time to do all this stuff? It's actually a great question and, just like every other step I've taken in my career, I've found the answer through a series of backward and forward steps. Many authors will answer you by saying that you have to write more than you market and that's true, but I'm going to take it one step further. I'm going to share my system with you and detail how to find your balance between writing and non-writing duties.

During 2013 I wrote and published three new books: a collection of short stories, *Lies I Never Told*; a romance novel, *Believing Again: A Tale of Two Christmases*; and the original version of the book you're reading, *How I Sold 30,000 eBooks on Amazon's Kindle – An Easy-To-Follow Self-Publishing Guidebook*. I was pleased with my output. My writing/marketing ratio was about 40/60. This was okay but I wanted it higher, especially when I read in Russell Blake's blog that he'd written and published twenty-four books in the previous three years. Russell is another of the big guns in Indie publishing. He's found a genre that his readers enjoy, and he's written some great books. He also co-wrote a book with legendary author Clive Cussler. So, Russell is doing well. He claims to live by a 70/30 writing to marketing ratio. In these calculations, by the way, we're including all non-writing activities that are associated with publishing as part of the marketing number. So, Russell is creating new material for his readers seventy percent of the time that he's working (which I suspect is most of his non-sleeping time.) That's huge and I was very impressed, but I knew I couldn't get there. I didn't think I could just turn a switch and make the change. I wanted to increase the amount of time I was devoting to writing without sacrificing any of the other tasks that are associated with being a self-published author. I needed to take it step by step.

Here are the steps I utilized:

1. **Determine a Ratio and Choose a Target.**
2. **Make a Pledge to Write a Set Number of New Words Daily.**
3. **Make a Pledge to Revise or Rewrite a Set Number of Words Daily.**
4. **Maintain and Re-Examine.**

1. Determine a Ratio and Choose a Target

Each time I've released a book, I've put less work into the production, publishing, and marketing aspects. The time spent on the creative process has either stayed the same or been longer. This is a good thing. My aim is to become a better writer, and each time I publish a new book I want readers to comment on my maturity as a writer. I want them to know that each time they purchase my work they are guaranteed a professional product, not just in terms of presentation but also in terms of content. With some minor exceptions, the process I've gone through to produce my product (beta reading, editing, cover design, and writing blurbs), and publish my work (formatting, uploading, and utilizing Amazon's tools), has remained the same. The marketing aspect has changed only in terms of where I've promoted my book. New outlets appear from time to time, and if my support group has given the site the green light or if I wish to experiment, I'll try to reach readers by submitting to them. So, the peripheral duties, the non-writing tasks, have taken less time with each book I've produced, and I've been able to devote more time to writing. Before reaching step two and increasing my output, I had achieved a ratio of 40/60. That means I was writing forty percent of the time. This was an incremental increase and it happened because I became more efficient with each book. In other words I was following the steps outlined in this guidebook and had learned from my mistakes. My ratio of 40/60 wasn't bad, but I wanted to create more books. Like you, I want to be one of the writers who are referred to as *successful self-published authors*. To reach that next step, I needed to set a target.

I believe in challenges and finding the next mountain to climb, but I also believe in targeting achievable goals. I felt if I could reach a 50/50 ratio, devoting half of my working time to writing, it would be a big step. For this step I needed to increase my writing output by ten percent, while not sacrificing the efforts I was putting into the other duties.

2. Make a Pledge to Write a Set Number of New Words Daily

I really like numbers. I like that they don't change. So, I picked a number—1,000—and decided I'd write 1,000 new words each day. No matter what. Then I wrote a blog for Indies Unlimited detailing how I was going to do it. I called the article the 1,000 Words a Day Project:

www.indiesunlimited.com/2014/02/04/the-1000-words-a-day-project/

It was a project, but it was a pledge too. And, by blogging about it on a heavy-traffic site like IU, I knew I'd have to follow up. I knew that somewhere along the line someone would email or message me and ask whether I was still writing 1,000 new words a day, every day. I established some rules for my challenge:

A. I must write a minimum of 1,000 words a day. Excess amounts can be carried over, but if the target isn't met, the initiative is over and must be restarted. For example, 1,500 words written on Monday means I only need 500 words on Tuesday. And, 900 words written on Monday means I must start over.

B. To qualify, words written must be new words. Words written during rewriting, revising, or editing are not considered part of the daily target.

C. I must not pester other authors who are participating in their own 1,000 words a day project. I can briefly compare notes, but I will not draw them in or allow myself to be drawn into long, protracted conversations which inevitably turn to which social network is the bomb and whether free promotions still work.

D. My workday is over when I go to sleep. So, it is acceptable to complete my daily word target at 3 a.m. the following morning. The moment my head hits my pillow for my evening slumber the day has ended.

E. Words can be written for any project that I aim to publish: poetry, self-help, fiction, blogs for Indies Unlimited or my website, anything. As long as my motivation is to publish the work, the words will count. Words written for a non-related day job do not qualify.

F. Gibberish qualifies. I've begun writing exercises with gibberish and ended up with either a good idea or a paragraph or two that's usable. I'm a writer. If I start with gibberish it should end up as something else. As long as there are 1,000 new words on the page, the target has been met.

It's difficult to follow through on a pledge like this but once I established some routines and changed my habits, it became easier. At first though, it was difficult.

The problem with committing to a challenge is that life can get in the way. Like everyone else, I have a busy life filled with commitments, some of which I have control over, some of which my significant other controls for me. There were evenings where I was so tired that I held my hand under my chin and typed with the other hand to reach those thousand words. Now, I plan ahead. If I have an event coming up I accumulate words, and almost every night in our home I'm asked, "Have you done your words yet?"

The one thousand words a day pledge has become a part of my life. Since its inception I've produced additional blog posts, a thirty thousand-word novella, and I've written significant portions of my two upcoming novels. Plus, I've added sections to the book you're currently reading. The additional blog posts I've accumulated mean that I've been able to contribute articles to an editors association's website, the B.R.A.G. (Book Readers Group Medallion) site, *The Write Place at the Write Time* online magazine, and several other prominent sites. This has been an additional benefit of the pledge.

3. Make a Pledge to Revise or Rewrite a Set Number of Words Daily

After a while, writing one thousand words a day will come naturally. For me, I know that it has to happen before I can go to bed. It has become part of my regular routine. At this point I will suggest to you that if you cannot commit to one thousand words pick a lesser amount. Target five hundred or three hundred or even one hundred words. It doesn't matter the amount. Once you hit your stride you can always increase. Make the target attainable. Look after yourself. There's no point in becoming frustrated and giving up.

Once I felt comfortable hitting my daily target, I examined the other areas that make up my job description as a writer. I'd run several successful promotions during the time frame, and I didn't feel as though I'd missed any opportunities. I'd continued to encourage and learn from my support group. I'd made small changes to my product presentation in order to stimulate sales during the challenge period. One area was lacking though: I had done very little rewriting or revising. Other than rewriting blogs before submitting them, I'd neglected the drafts of my novels and the completed projects that I'd worked so hard on. I almost felt a physical pain pulling me back, beckoning me to revise. I couldn't, though. I felt that I didn't have time. So, when I got to the point where writing the new words was a comfortable and attainable task, I added to the challenge.

I amended the pledge to include revising or rewriting two thousand words every day. This part was easy. I wanted to do it—badly. I had first drafts of chapters and a somewhat completed story that I was aching to get to. The first day that I tackled the revising in addition to the new words, I overshot by three thousand words. It felt great that I had been able to revisit work that had been dormant. The obvious advantage was that some of it had been untouched for a few weeks and going back with a totally fresh perspective was golden. So, the third part of my strategy calculated to achieve a balance meant that I would revise or rewrite two thousand (already written) words each day. Believe me, this part is easy. You'll want to do it, and you will find the time. I wrote a follow up article for Indies

Unlimited **www.indiesunlimited.com/2014/05/20/the-1000-words-a-day-project-the-10002000-pledge/** detailing how I amended my challenge. This was how I turned it into a pledge. If you say you're going to do something, and you write about it online, somebody at some point is going to call you on it. It's pressure, but it's good pressure too.

4. Maintain and Re-Examine

My initial target of one thousand new words each day was, at times, a tough climb. Working it in increments and building up to one thousand would have been easier. Fortunately it worked out for me, and I'm now at a point where the new words and the revised work are part of my daily life. I often get to the point where I'm three or four thousand words ahead, and then I fall back to zero and need to put the time in again to accumulate and get ahead. In adding step three, and revising as well as writing new words, I have now attained a 60/40 ratio. Sixty percent of my working time is spent writing. I'm comfortable with this split, and at this point I don't foresee myself increasing the ratio. There is one very important factor to consider as you undertake this challenge. Please take careful note of the next paragraph.

Set realistic targets, and if you fail to initially meet your goal, start again at a lower number. It doesn't matter what it is. As mentioned previously, try one hundred words a day, and when that's become part of your workday, increase it. Do not give up. You've written, or are close to completing, a book. You created a work from the voices in your head (or that's how I do it anyway). Your goal is to be a self-published author and connect with readers. In order to do this you need targets, but you also need to put yourself in a position to hit those targets. For this step do not compare yourself with anyone else. We all have very different lives. I know a lady who has six children. She gets up at four a.m. every morning to write. The kids are up at five thirty. She does this five days a week and has followed this schedule for years. That may not work for you. You might only be able to devote thirty minutes a day. It doesn't matter. Thirty minutes a day of writing is more writing than ninety-nine percent of the population is doing. Find a target, follow the above steps, and achieve your target (whatever it is). And, when you've achieved it, congratulate yourself and of course, try to maintain it.

With my 60/40 ratio, I've achieved a workable balance. It's not always easily attainable, but it's something I feel I can do every day. I examine my writing versus non-writing duties at the end of every month in much the same way a small company might have a staff meeting to assess how they're running their business. If I ever felt that I had a month of personal events coming up, or there was some other obstacle in my path, I'd adjust my numbers down and try to hit that target every day. Don't be hard on yourself, achieve your goals, maintain them, and adjust as necessary.

When I turn on my computer, the first file I open is my "Daily Word Count" document. This details whether I'm ahead or behind in meeting my personal pledge. Whereas at first it seemed like I was adding a new anxiety, now it's become a part of my daily routine. And it's eliminated the anxiety of wondering whether or not I'm writing enough. From time to time I'll see other authors experiencing great success and after jumping up and down and being happy for them, I'll wonder whether I'm doing enough to try to get there. That's part of our competitive instinct and it's normal. I can refer to my daily word list and reassure myself that I'm writing and creating and moving toward completing another book. By this point you might be feeling overwhelmed and wondering how you're going to complete all the work I've given you throughout this book. You're going to do it by formulating your own personal balance and not comparing your output to anyone else's. The next step, the steps I've been suggesting throughout these chapters, is to run your writing career as though it were a small business. The steps I've given you will allow you to do this. Take them gradually. Keep living and don't shut out the entire outside world. If you're reading this book, then you're committed to your work, and my experience is that if you've made this kind of commitment, you've probably written a great book. There are readers for great books. Establish a balance and perform the tasks when you have time. Adapt the numbers to suit your lifestyle and enjoy the journey. Once you begin connecting with readers, you'll realize that it's all been worth it.

CHAPTER TWELVE HOMEWORK

1. Determine how much writing you're doing in a day and how much non-writing business type work you're doing. Estimate what the percentage of writing/marketing (non-creative writing) you're accomplishing.
2. Set a goal. What ratio fits your current lifestyle? What's attainable? Pick a ratio number and a number of words per day that you can comfortably and consistently write. Record it on your daily word count document.
3. Once you've hit your groove and are producing your goal, add the amount of words you're going to revise or rewrite daily.
4. Take it easy on yourself and adjust as necessary. Keep living!

CHAPTER ELEVEN FOLLOW-UP

1. How is your media kit looking? Does it need to be updated?
2. Are your schedules working for you or do they need to be adjusted?
3. Have you found some help? Are you staying within your budget?

CHAPTER THIRTEEN
THE FINISH LINE

Up until a slew of injuries, I spent much of my non-writing time training for races with a group of friends. We would complete training runs once or twice a week, and we participated in several races a year. There's a huge amount of satisfaction in crossing that finish line, especially if you've trained correctly and reached your goal time. I'm experiencing a similar feeling right now. We've just gone through the work together. You've done the hard work—you wrote the book—and I've shown you the things that worked for me. Although in reaching the end of this book we've crossed a finish line of sorts, I'm sorry to have to tell you that the first discussion my friends and I have, after completing a race, is determining where our next race or challenge is going to be. So, as Winston Churchill said, "Now this is not the end. It is not even the beginning of the end. But it is perhaps, the end of the beginning."

Didn't that sound dramatic? I thought so, too. My point is, just as writing is a skill that needs to be practiced and learned and relearned and never perfected, finding a way to reach your readers is somewhat the same. In the years since I released my book, many things have changed, and I've had to change with them. When *My Temporary Life* caught fire and was selling thousands of copies, I was exposed to lots of different people. Because of this exposure, I was emailed by folks from all over the world asking me what the secret sauce was. As you know by now, the answer quite simply is that there is no secret sauce. The only secret is that it's hard work, luck, being open and alert to new ideas, adhering to a philosophy of helping others, and conducting your business in a professional and efficient manner (as outlined in this book). And, of course, producing a book that readers want to read.

In closing I'll share one final story with you. My self-publishing journey has introduced me to people I'd never otherwise have had the opportunity to meet. I've become friends with an Emmy Award-winning actor/producer, an Olympian gold medalist, and a whole lot of incredibly talented authors. Many of them have become very close friends. None of them have touched me or my family as deeply as David McColl has.

David contacted me after my story came out in the *Globe and Mail* newspaper. David lives in eastern Canada and emailed me because he'd written a self-help book and was contemplating hiring a company to help him self-publish. The dollar amounts the company quoted him were very high. David titled his book *A Father's Tears,* and it's the story of how he lost his son in an accident and how he dealt with his grief afterward. David's son, Tony, was driving friends home from a party when his car was hit by another vehicle that was driving erratically. Tony and the other driver were both killed. Tony had not been drinking; he'd simply been driving his friends home. Tragically, Tony was only nineteen when he lost his life, and even at that young age, he was already a beloved figure in the community. Some of Tony's friends formed *Tony's Promise,* an organization that helps friends keep friends off the road if they've been drinking. All of this was in its infancy when David contacted me and sent me his book. Today, there are thousands of members of *Tony's Promise.*

David wrote a very, very good book. Somehow, in spite of the horrendous circumstances he was living through, he managed to write a book that has the potential to help a lot of people, and although it's written primarily for men, it certainly has the power to help both men and women. When David called me and sent me a copy of his manuscript, it was one of the privileges of my life to tell him that he wouldn't need to hire a company or pay someone money to self-publish his book.

David released his book in late 2012, and I don't know how many copies of *A Father's Tears* he's sold, but I know that every time someone downloads his book it has the potential to save a life.

This is a wonderful industry we're in, and it's a great time to be a writer. I hope you find lots of readers and sell lots of books and continue to write, and remember, don't give up. If your book hasn't found its feet yet, then go back and write another one. It's truly that simple. We're writers first and publishers/marketers/promoters second. This book isn't about teaching you how to write; it's about teaching you how to present the most professional product possible and how to find the most efficient road to those sometimes-elusive readers. If it hasn't worked this time then you (and I) must go back to the beginning and write another book, because as that panel of bestselling writers told me years ago, we all need to keep trying to perfect our craft and become better writers. I wish you well.

CHAPTER FOURTEEN
KINDLE SCOUT: THE GAME-CHANGER
OR
A Three Dressed Up as a Nine

And then everything changed. Or, as I already said, things continued to change. Nothing stood still. At the beginning of 2016 it was easier to get your words onto the electronic page than it ever had been before. Anyone could now be a writer. Anyone could publish a book on Kindle and see his or her words on Amazon's product pages. But, not everyone was connecting with readers. Not every book was finding an audience.

There have been some extraordinary books published by self-published authors in the last five years. There are some very talented writers out there, and many have established a large following. They have their work professionally edited, employ a talented cover designer, and launch their book with a bang. Then there are others who have great covers and awful content. There are some really bad books out there. I know this because I've bought some of them. I read an enticing blurb, click on the compelling cover, and (after neglecting to read the "look inside" feature) purchase the book. Then, when I'm tucked in with my Kindle I read opening sentences that are actually full paragraphs, half-stories that have no antagonist (and barely a protagonist), and clichéd ramblings that reads like very bad television. Not everyone is working at his or her craft in the same manner as you and I. Our poor readers are often duped into believing that if it's on Amazon, it's worthy of their discretionary dollars. I'm sorry to say that often this is not the case.

As I scroll the product pages, I can see that in the past thirty days there were almost one hundred thousand e-books released on amazon.com. There are approximately four million e-books available to Amazon customers today. Unfortunately, some of the authors of those books have disguised their unfinished, insufficient prose with smart-looking covers, and their blurbs read like they've been written by snake oil salesman. I'm not referring to books that my high-brow taste turns its nose up at, yet sell well. I realize that for every *Wool* there's a *Fifty Shades*. I mean the real stinkers. What is a reader to do? How can they wade through the grade-school-standard books and reach the quality, entertaining literature? And, more importantly for you and I, how can authors of quality, entertaining literature stand out from the crowd and show the reading public that our work deserves to be considered?

By mid-2015 my book sales had once again stalled. I had published five books under my own name and two under a pen name through a small publisher. I completed a new book that I'd been working on for three years – ***The Dead List (A John Drake Mystery)***. I had this amazing concept in my head – what if a group of friends took life insurance policies out on each other and then waited to cash in? Then, what if they started dying, suspiciously, one by one? I decided to work the plot around a character that I'd been formulating for a while – an over-age, rookie cop with a mysterious past who was stationed in a small town. It was a new genre for me, but after being a fan of Henning Mankell et al for years, I felt like I'd found my groove. I was meant to write mysteries. I found some beta readers who were huge mystery fans, and I managed to find some police personnel who were happy to help me with terminology and procedural details that I may have gotten wrong. The police helped me make several corrections (several meaning many). Then when the beta readers read the revised versions, their feedback was beyond what I had expected. They loved the book. Almost all of them had not known who the murderer was until the end, and all of them wanted to read more stories featuring the same character. Mission accomplished. Now all I had to do was find a way to make my new book stand out from all those other books. I was back at the beginning again. Almost.

I have a small but extremely loyal following that I knew would check out my work no matter what I wrote, so I knew I'd have an initial spike on the rankings chart and perhaps hit the Hot New Releases list. But beyond that I didn't know what I'd do. I had a friend who spent just under one thousand dollars on her launch and saw her book hit top ten overall, but when it fell, it fell fast. The cliff that we've spoken of happens very quickly now. There is very little lag time. When our book sales shift from the hundreds each day to the teens and less, the rankings move us further and further away from the top of the pile almost immediately. I knew that by using the methods illustrated in the previous chapters of this book I'd make a run for the upper echelons of the rankings, but I wanted to try something different with this novel.

I'd been reading about Amazon's Kindle Scout program for a few months, and a couple of friends had been successful Scout campaigners. Here's how it works. You submit your edited manuscript to Kindle Scout with a bio and your book cover. If the Scout editors feel it's a book their readers may be interested in, you are granted the opportunity to run a Kindle Scout campaign. For thirty days your book cover, bio, and the first section (usually a chapter, sometimes a little longer) are displayed on the Kindle Scout landing page. As of this writing the accepted genres are: Literary Fiction; Mystery; Thriller and Suspense; Romance; Science Fiction and Fantasy; and Teen and Young Adult. If readers think your book is worthy of publication, they nominate it, and if it wins, they receive a free copy. If you have enough votes, your book will be shown in the "Hot and Trending" list at the top of the page.

At the end of the thirty days, you're shown your statistics. You'll see how many hours you spent in Hot and Trending, the percentage breakdown of where your nominations came from (generated by you or by Scout), and where your traffic came from (Facebook posts, email blast, etc.). If you've made enough of a splash, then the Scout editors will consider publishing your book through Kindle Press. They can take up to ten days to decide, and if you make it to the other side, you're offered a contract for e-book, audio, and foreign rights. The contract is for five years, offers a 50% royalty rate and a $1,500 advance.

Kindle Press is an Amazon imprint. They don't have the clout to generate traffic to your book like some of the other imprints (Thomas and Mercer, Lake Union, etc.), but they have the potential to get more eyeballs on your book than you or I can generate. And there's a guarantee of sorts. If you don't receive $5,000 annually for the five years of the contract you can opt out and the rights revert back to you. Plus, if they decide not to publish you and you release the book yourself, Amazon will notify all the readers who voted for you when your book goes live. I've seen authors have very successful launches after not being accepted by Scout.

So, two questions come immediately: is there an effective way to run a Scout campaign that will help win a contract, and if accepted, is it worthwhile to let them publish you? I can and will answer both of those questions for you.

I heavily researched Scout before my campaign, and I had the luxury of quizzing my friends who had run successful campaigns. I read every blog and article I could find on how to maximize your chances. You don't have to do that because you have me. I wrote of my Scout campaign for (yes, those guys again), Indies Unlimited. It's a two-part article. You can check it out here:

www.indiesunlimited.com/2015/10/13/my-kindle-scout-adventure-part-1/

Please read it because it's important that you are able to access the groups that will help you, and it's good to see what worked and what did not. The very short version is—spread your efforts out over the course of the thirty days, Facebook posts worked best for me, an email blast to my followers was also effective, and don't stress. My personal research (and some guesswork) indicates that the editors are interested in seeing the percentage of traffic generated by the author close to the percentage generated from the Scout landing page. There probably a minimum number of nominations and hours in Hot and Trending that are required (this number is not disclosed of course), but there have been campaigns with fewer nominations that were still offered a contract. This goes back to the basic premise of this book—produce an entertaining, professional product and you will find an audience. Or in this case, you will attract the attention of the editors.

I submitted **The Dead List** to Kindle Scout. They accepted my book, and one day after the thirty days had expired they offered me a contract. To try to make myself feel even more special, I researched the approximately seventy authors who had already been accepted at that point to see if I was the first non-American author. This was to use in my marketing material and had nothing to do with ego of course. There were other non-Americans, so this did not help me. But I was very happy to be part of the group of talented authors whose books had made it through. Scout signed me up and assigned me an editor. As you know, my books are professionally copyedited, so there were no errors found. There was a procedural point that the editor questioned and I made the correction. They did have some thoughts on my cover though.

My original cover showed a police officer on a dark street standing over a dead body. The Scout contact person suggested removing the body in order to "qualify for all of Amazon's promotional opportunities." Enough said. The body was removed. Once I submitted the revised cover and manuscript I received my advance within days, and the book was released about a month later along with five other Scout winners. The launch and first two months were less than impressive. I was able to watch my rankings, but there is a two-month lag on receiving sales numbers. From the ranking chart (that is provided earlier in this book) I could make a fairly good guess on how many books I was selling. Bear in mind that your followers who have nominated your book receive a free copy, so that revenue stream has disappeared. The upside is that we now have an arm of Amazon working to find new readers for our books. In the first month I sold 170 books. In month two I sold about the same. I was fairly confident I could have had a more successful launch if I'd published the book myself.

I emailed my contact at Scout and asked what their promotional plans were for my book so that I could perhaps do something to complement their efforts. They told me they would be featuring my book in a January promotion aimed at avid readers. When that happened, everything began to make sense. During the January promo, my book sat below the 10,000 overall ranking point almost all month. For the last two weeks of the promotion it was anywhere from 600 overall to 5,000. So in month three I earned my advance back and began to make some money. In month four, as the promotion wound down I had my strongest month (with this book) so far. The Scout folks, who are actually the Kindle Press folks, tell me that each published book receives three major promotional opportunities in the first year. Plus every time my book is part of a promotion I just sit back and watch the numbers; they do the heavy lifting. Kindle Press pays the advertising costs to get the word out. By the way, one of the sites they use to promote our books is BookBub. I'll bet you thought you wouldn't have to read about them again in this book.

I'm so encouraged by the relationship I have with Kindle Press and the number of readers that I'm connecting with that I will probably submit my next book to them too. For me this is the next step. If you write in a series and are releasing book two or three in the series, they will consider the middle book in a series for a Scout campaign. I have a colleague who released book three of her series through Kindle Press after self-publishing the first two books. After publication the sales of the other books in the series spiked up too. Another colleague recently signed a three-book print deal with a major traditional publisher based on the exposure her e-book received by being published by Kindle Press.

I hope you go through the process outlined in the preceding chapters and do the work and connect with readers. It's an incredibly satisfying experience to do it yourself. And, although I'm ending this book showing you a shortcut of sorts (it would be remiss of me to not point out all of the opportunities available to you), to submit to Scout you will still require a professional cover, editing, synopsis, and more, so the methods we have been working on are still necessary.

There's a Scottish saying that I'm fond of. Imagine me telling you in my Scottish accent: "You do the digging and I'll hold your jacket." I hope I've done that for you adequately in the chapters of this book. I'll hand you back your jacket now and wish you a creative, productive year, and we'll do this all again in a year or so from now.

HELPFUL LINKS
AND
MARTIN'S MEDIA KIT

HELPFUL BLOGS AND SITES TO FOLLOW
martincrosbie.com/
www.indiesunlimited.com/
jakonrath.blogspot.ca/
www.hughhowey.com/
amandahocking.blogspot.ca/
www.bidinotto.com/
russellblake.com/

QUERY TRACKER
querytracker.net

NATIONAL NOVEL WRITING MONTH
www.NaNoWriMo.org/

SOCIAL NETWORK SITES
www.facebook.com
www.goodreads.com
https://twitter.com/
www.linkedin.com/
www.wattpad.com/
https://www.blogger.com/
www.stumbleupon.com/

https://www.pinterest.com/
https://www.tumblr.com/
https://www.instagram.com/

PREDITORS AND EDITORS, ABSOLUTE WRITE, AND WRITER BEWARE

pred-ed.com/
absolutewrite.com/forums/index.php
www.sfwa.org/other-resources/for-authors/writer-beware/

FORUMS AND GROUPS

https://kdp.amazon.com/community/index.jspa
www.kboards.com/
groups.yahoo.com/
www.amazon.com/forum/meet%20our%20authors
absolutewrite.com/forums/index.php

KINDLE SCOUT

kindlescout.amazon.com/

EDITORS

Laurie Boris laurieboris@earthlink.net (Martin's editor)
Nicole Bouchard illuminedessenceediting.weebly.com/my-
  approach--about-me.html
K. S. Brooks ksbrooks@ksbrooks.com

BETA-READERS

www.indiesunlimited.com/resource-beta-readers/

WEBSITE ASSISTANT
Faith Mondigo faytebuds03@gmail.com

BOOK COVER AWARDS
www.thebookdesigner.com/2011/08/monthly-e-book-cover-design-awards/

PHOTO-MODIFICATION SITES
picasa.google.com/
www.gimp.org/
www.getpaint.net/

ROYALTY-FREE PHOTO SITES
www.visualphotos.com
www.bigstockphoto.com
imageshack.us
www.freedigitalphotos.net/images/about.php

FREE PHOTOS AND IMAGES
Please check each site's guidelines and ensure that the photo you're using is copyright-free.
NYPL Public Domain publicdomain.nypl.org/pd-
   visualization/#sthash.zh03YJ4C.dpuf
Alegri Photos www.alegriphotos.com/
Animal Photos animalphotos.info/a/
British Library (Flickr)
   https://www.flickr.com/photos/britishlibrary
Cepolina Photos www.cepolina.com/freephoto/
Death To The Stock Photo deathtothestockphoto.com/

Digital Comic Museum digitalcomicmuseum.com/index.php

Dreamstime www.dreamstime.com/free-photos

Every Stock Photo www.everystockphoto.com/

Flickr Creative Commons
  https://www.flickr.com/creativecommons/

Free Digital Photos www.freedigitalphotos.net/

Free Foto www.freefoto.com/index.jsp

Free Images www.freeimages.com/

Free Images Live www.freeimageslive.co.uk/

Free Pixels www.freepixels.com/

Free Stock Photos www.freestockphotos.mobi/

Google Creative Commons
  www.google.com/advanced_image_search?hl=en

Image Base www.imagebase.net/

Kave Wall www.kavewall.com/stock/

Morgue File morguefile.com/

Open Photo openphoto.net/

Photo Gen www.photogen.com/

Photo Vaco www.photovaco.com/

Pic Jumbo picjumbo.com/

Pixabay pixabay.com/en/

Public Domain Archive publicdomainarchive.com/us/

School Photo Project www.schoolphotoproject.com/

Stick Stock Photos www.stickstock.com/#

Stock Pholio stockpholio.com/

Stock Photos stockphotos.io/

Super Famous superfamous.com/

Sun Pix www.sunipix.com/

Toasto www.toasto.com/

Viintage **viintage.com/**
Wikimedia Commons
  commons.wikimedia.org/wiki/Main_Page

BOOK COVERS

extendedimagery.com
www.romancenovelcovers.com
Jun Ares aresjun@gmail.com (Martin's cover designer)

FORMATTING

calibre-ebook.com/ (do-it-yourself)
quantumformatting.weebly.com/ (Rich Meyer's formatting site)

LISTS OF REVIEWERS/BLOGGERS AND REVIEW SITES

www.amazon.com/review/top-reviewers
www.stepbystepselfpublishing.net/reviewer-list.html
www.theindieview.com/indie-reviewers/
www.gregscowen.com/2012/02/a-few-indie-book-reviewers/
www.tweetyourbooks.com/#!free-reviews/c1yij
https://www.thekindlebookreview.net/book-reviews/
triskelebooks.blogspot.co.uk/2013/03/indie-friendly-book-
  reviewers.html
indiebookreviewer.wordpress.com/index/
pippajay.blogspot.ca/p/blog-page_14.html
www.mediabistro.com/galleycat/best-book-reviewers-on-
  twitter_b11136
www.midwestbookreview.com/links/othr_rev.htm

www.indiesunlimited.com/reviews-and-review-sites/

HELPFUL ARTICLES

www.indiesunlimited.com/2012/03/17/helping-you-become-a-1-bestselling-author/

www.indiesunlimited.com/2013/03/07/buylike-my-bookpagewebsite/

www.indiesunlimited.com/2013/05/31/how-to-find-the-picture-when-you-already-got-the-picture-reverse-image-searching-made-easy/

www.indiesunlimited.com/2013/07/02/for-the-love-of-the-book/

www.indiesunlimited.com/2014/05/20/the-1000-words-a-day-project-the-10002000-pledge/

www.indiesunlimited.com/2015/10/13/my-kindle-scout-adventure-part-1/

DISTRIBUTION AND PUBLISHING PLATFORMS

www.smashwords.com/

https://kdp.amazon.com/self-publishing/signin

PROMOTIONAL SITES FOR YOUR FREE AND DISCOUNTED BOOKS

ereadernewstoday.com/

buckbooks.net/buck-books-promotions/#

www.pixelofink.com/

www.peoplereads.com/

www.booktastik.com/

www.fkbooksandtips.com/for-authors/free-kindle-book-

submission-form/
home.bookbub.com/home/
www.indiesunlimited.com/freebie-friday/_(now called Thrifty Thursdays)
freeebooksdaily.net/
freedigitalreads.com/
freebooksy.com/
kindlenationdaily.com/
www.worldliterarycafe.com/content/find-your-books-wings
bargainbooksy.com/sell-more-books/
kindlemojo.com/
www.totallyfreestuff.com/
www.icravefreebies.com/contact/
fireapps.blogspot.ca/p/app-developers-authors.html
www.freebookdude.com/p/list-your-free-book.html
blog.booksontheknob.org/about-this-blog-and-contact-info
freebooksy.com/editorial-submissions
www.thatbookplace.com/free-promo-submissions/
addictedtoebooks.com/submission
bookgorilla.com/
www.kindleboards.com/free-book-promo/
indiebookoftheday.com/authors/free-on-kindle-listing/
www.ebooklister.net/submit.php
kindlebookpromos.luckycinda.com/?page_id=283
thedigitalinkspot.blogspot.com.es/p/contact-us.html
ereaderutopia.com/
www.freeebooksdaily.com/
www.freebookshub.com/authors/
www.frugal-freebies.com/

www.ereaderiq.com/about/
askdavid.com/free-book-promotion
ebookshabit.com/about-us/
www.ereaderperks.com/about/
snickslist.com/books/place-ad/
awesomegang.com/submit-your-book/
thefrugalereader.wufoo.com/forms/frugal-freebie-submissions/
www.goodkindles.net/p/why-should-i-submit-my-book-
here.html
www.blackcaviar-bookclub.com/free-book-
promotion.html#.UXFB27XYeOc
digitalbooktoday.com/12-top-100-submit-your-free-book-to-
be-included-on-this-list/
www.kornerkonnection.com/index.html?fb=ebookkornerkafe
www.dailycheapreads.com/
bookgoodies.com/submit-your-free-kindle-days/highlight-
your-free-kindle-days/
bookgoodies.com/bargain-books/kdp-countdown-bargain-
books/
indiebookoftheday.com
pixelscroll.com/feature-your-product-2/
www.thefussylibrarian.com/for-authors/
www.ebookbargainsuk.com/price.html
www.humanmade.net/submission-form
www.ebooksoda.com/
www.theereadercafe.com/
www.orangeberrybooktours.com/
www.bookblast.co/advertise/advertise.php
choosybookworm.com/authors/

www.bookbear.info/

https://www.themidlist.com/

readingdeals.com/

www.masqueradecrew.com/2014/10/advertising-options-from-masquerade-crew.html

www.ebookstage.com/authorAreaPage.xhtml

newfreekindlebooks.com/authors/

https://www.facebook.com/onlyromance (Facebook Group)

https://www.facebook.com/ebooksfreefreefree___ (Facebook Group)

https://www.facebook.com/pages/UK-Kindle-Book-Lovers/175617412524192 (Facebook Group)

https://www.facebook.com/kindle (Facebook Group)

https://www.facebook.com/pages/The-Frugal-eReader/101086513289732 (Facebook Group)

https://www.facebook.com/pages/Short-Stories-Flash-Fiction-Stories/692915047420207 (Facebook Page)

https://www.facebook.com/BookJunkiesLibrary (Facebook Group)

https://www.facebook.com/IndieKindleWLC (Facebook Group)

https://www.facebook.com/weloveebooks (Facebook Group)

https://www.facebook.com/Bargain.eBook.Hunter (Facebook Group)

https://www.facebook.com/TheKindleObsessed (Facebook Group)

https://www.facebook.com/KindleNation (Facebook Group)

https://www.facebook.com/ebookimpresario (Facebook Group)

https://www.facebook.com/earthsbooknook (Facebook Group)

https://www.facebook.com/AontheC (Facebook Group)

https://www.facebook.com/iauthor?sk=wall (Facebook Group)

https://www.facebook.com/kuforum (Facebook Group)

https://www.facebook.com/IndieBookLounge___ (Facebook Group)

https://www.facebook.com/DigitalBookAddicts (Facebook Group)

https://www.facebook.com/groups/602196313230557/ - for Kindle Unlimited titles

https://www.facebook.com/groups/1485322851757071/ - Free Short Reads (short stories and flash fiction)

https://www.facebook.com/groups/etotallyfree/ - Totally Free eBooks

https://www.facebook.com/groups/freekindlebookclub/ - Free Kindle Books

https://www.facebook.com/groups/Bookjunkiesfreebies/ - Book Junkies Freebies

uk.hundredzeros.com/ (UK site)

freekindlefiction.blogspot.co.uk/ (UK site)

flurriesofwords.blogspot.co.uk/ (UK site)

ebookdealoftheday.co.uk/submissions/ (UK site)

www.dailycheapreads.co.uk/ (UK site)

www.indie-book-bargains.co.uk (UK site)

pretty-hot.com/submit-your-book/ (erotica only)

wantonreads.com/tell-us-about-your-book/ (erotica only)

www.kornerkonnection.com/index.html?fbkornerkafex (erotica only)

www.xtme.de/submitting-a-free-e-book-to-xtmeenglishbooks/

(German site for English books)

CONVENIENT LISTS OF PROMOTIONAL SITES
authormarketingclub.com/members/submit-your-book/
authormarketingclub.com/members/amc-paid-promo-book-list/
www.authorpreneurmagazine.com/72-places-to-promote-your-kindle-book-when-its-free/
www.ebookbooster.com/ **(they have a list of sites on their home page)**

PAID SERVICES THAT SUBMIT YOUR BOOK
ebookbooster.com/
bookpraiser.com/

PODCASTS
www.blogtalkradio.com/

TWITTER ACCOUNTS TO NOTIFY DURING YOUR PROMOTION
@kindlenews
@DigitalBkToday
@kindleebooks
@Kindlestuff
@KindleEbooksUK
@KindleBookKing
@KindleFreeBook
@Freebookdude
@Kindlefinds

@Kindlebookreview
@free
@free_kindle
@FreeReadFeed
@4FreeKindleBook
@FreeKindleStuff
@KindleUpdates
@kindleebooks
@Kindlestuff
@kindlesfnovel
@kindlemysbook
@Kindle_Freebies
@hashltrd
@100freebooks
@kindletop100
@kindleowners
@IndAuthorSucess
@FreeEbooksDaily
@AwesometasticBk
@Bookyrnextread
@Kindle_promo
@CheapKindleDly
@KindleDaily
@BookBub

HASHTAGS TO USE DURING PROMOTION

richlycoloredmask.blogspot.co.uk/2012/10/twitter-hashtags-for-writers.html

#free

#freekindle
#freebook
#kindlepromo
#freeebook

SALES RANKING CALCULATION
www.theresaragan.com/p/sale-ranking-chart.html

GOOGLE ALERTS AND MENTION
www.google.com/alerts
https://en.mention.net/

AMAZON'S TOOLS
www.amazon.com
www.authorcentral.amazon.com
www.goodreads.com/
https://affiliate-program.amazon.com/

CATEGORIES, TAGS AND KEYWORDS
https://kdp.amazon.com/self-
publishing/help?topicId=A200PDGPEIQX41
https://kdp.amazon.com/self-
publishing/help?topicId=A2EZES9JAJ6H02&ref=23&ref_=
pe_390220_32492950

LINK SHORTENING SITES
https://bitly.com/
tinyurl.com/

SAMPLE DMCA ABUSE LETTER

DMCA ABUSE: COPYRIGHT VIOLATION (request to remove files in violation):
[insert Date and Violating Website here]
Attn: (insert site contact person)

Pursuant to 17 USC 512(c)(3)(A), this communication serves as a statement that:
(1). I am [the exclusive rights holder for (insert book title and ISBN)

(2). These exclusive rights are being violated by material available upon your site at the following URL(s): (insert web address)

(3) I have a good faith belief that the use of this material in such a fashion is not authorized by the copyright holder, the copyright holder's agent, or the law;

(4) Under penalty of perjury in a United States court of law, I state that the information contained in this notification is accurate, and that I am authorized to act on the behalf of the exclusive rights holder for the material in question;

(5) I may be contacted by the following methods (include all): [physical address, telephone number, and email address];I hereby request that you remove or disable access to this material as it appears on your service in as expedient a fashion as possible.

Thank you for your kind cooperation.
    Regards,

SAMPLE DAILY WORDS SHEET

DAYS	DATE	PROJECT	NOTES	TODAY'S NEW	RUNNING TOTAL	TODAY'S REVISED	RUNNING TOTAL
1							
2							
3							
4							
5							
6							
7							
8							
9							
10							

MARTIN'S MEDIA KIT

In a press release, Amazon called Martin Crosbie's debut novel *My Temporary Life* one of their success stories. His self-publishing journey has been chronicled in *Publisher's Weekly*, *Forbes*, and Canada's *Globe and Mail* newspaper. Martin's recent release *The Dead List (A John Drake Mystery)* was awarded a publishing contract by Kindle Press.

He's also the author of *My Name Is Hardly - Book Two of the My Temporary Life Trilogy, Lies I Never Told - A Collection of Short Stories, How I Sold 30,000 eBooks on Amazon's Kindle - An Easy-To-Follow Self-Publishing Guidebook, 2016 Edition,* and *Believing Again: A Tale Of Two Christmases.*

Martin was born in the Highlands of Scotland and currently makes his home just outside Vancouver, on the west coast of Canada.

Martin's self-publishing journey has been documented here:

Publisher's Weekly Apr/2012 tinyurl.com/cq9ygdd

Globe and Mail newspaper Apr/2012 tinyurl.com/ks2v2e7
Forbes Aug/2012 tinyurl.com/gncrn8x

Martin is a proud contributor at Indies Unlimited:

www.indiesunlimited.com/author/martin-crosbie

Martin's Books:

The Dead List
(A John Drake Mystery)

Published Nov. 10, 2015
Publisher—Kindle Press
Mystery/Police Procedural
Amazon US **amzn.to/1WduUQQ**
Amazon UK **amzn.to/1RTUysK**
Amazon Canada **amzn.to/1YEewdS**

The dead man's head rests on a halo of blood. His hands are locked together as if in prayer. Rookie police officer John Drake is first on scene. His superiors want to call it an accidental death, but he isn't convinced. In his previous life, Drake saw his share of dead bodies. He knows this was not an accident. When he uncovers a list with five names including the name of the dead man, there's only one question. Are the names on the list suspects or potential victims?

What readers are saying about *The Dead List (A John Drake*

Mystery):

I thoroughly enjoyed reading this book, sometimes losing sleep just to finish the next chapter. If you love a good mystery you won't be disappointed. I can usually determine who the guilty party is, but I never saw this one coming! I'm so excited that this will be a series of books, and look forward to learning more about the mysterious John Drake. I have read Martin Crosbie's previous books, and loved them all, but this book takes the enjoyment to another level.

Kelly McRae (Amazon review)

Have you ever started reading a book that is so intriguing you don't want to put it down? Well this was that one for me. Even when I put it down I was always thinking about who was doing the murders. You aren't told until the end, so it keeps carrying you through the whole story. A very good read!

Sharon A. Brown (Amazon review)

My Temporary Life—**Book One of the My Temporary Life Trilogy**

MARTIN CROSBIE
MY TEMPORARY
LIFE

Book One of the
My Temporary Life
Trilogy

Published Dec. 19, 2011
Publisher—Martin Crosbie
Romantic Suspense
Available on Kindle
Amazon US tinyurl.com/l9xshv6
Amazon UK tinyurl.com/mxaxtlm
Amazon Canada tinyurl.com/lgpycef

Malcolm Wilson learns that everything is always temporary.

Growing up, he's raised by a promiscuous mother who can't stay out of trouble, his best friend is a thirteen-year-old alcoholic, and the masters at his tough Scottish school are always raising their canes in his direction. When he becomes an adult, he escapes, and chooses the safe route, watching the rest of the world from a distance. Everything changes the day he meets the beautiful, alluring, green-haired Heather, and when he learns of Heather's own abusive childhood and the horrific secret she's been carrying, Malcolm makes a decision—this time he's not backing down, whatever the cost.

The first book of the *My Temporary Life* Trilogy deals with friendship, love, and what it means to be a hero. It was a top-ten Amazon bestseller in all categories.

What readers are saying about *My Temporary Life:*
There were moments of magic, scenes filled with foreboding, passages that were poetic and ruminative, others that were breathtaking. The masterful handling of Malcolm's mother, was brilliant. There were many scenes, especially toward the end, that were fast-paced and made the book impossible to put down.
Susan Russo Anderson (Amazon review)

I have to say I have not read a book that took me on such an emotional ride in many years. I just finished it and I'm still reeling. I am typically a romance/fantasy reader but this is definitely going on my favorite books list. Martin Crosbie will be on my watch list of authors in the future. This was an incredible story to read.
Patricia Paonessa (Goodreads review)

Mr. Crosbie's first novel is a wonder! Once I started, I couldn't stop. I just HAD to find out what happened next. His characters are so believable and I felt a real connection to his hero's kind heart and the difficulties he faced while growing up and throughout his life. I completed the novel in just a day and was sad to have it end.

Flavia Joy (Amazon review)

My Name Is Hardly—**Book Two of the My Temporary Life Trilogy**

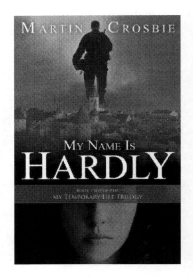

Published Dec. 10/2012
Publisher—Martin Crosbie
Historical Fiction
Available on Kindle
Amazon US tinyurl.com/jw7mf72
Amazon UK tinyurl.com/lkr3w3u
Amazon Canada tinyurl.com/n8hmu6u

A beautiful girl is missing, and may or may not want to be found, a soldier on his last and most dangerous mission, and a vow made to a dying friend. Northern Ireland, in 1996, was one of the most dangerous places in the world. The government called it a state of unrest, the people who lived through it called it the time of "The Troubles."

Gerald "Hardly" McDougall is a forgotten man. He's abused, bullied, and left behind. The only escape left is to join the British Army. At first, he's a reluctant soldier, then everything changes when tensions in Northern Ireland escalate and the Army needs a man with a particular set of characteristics. Hardly's re-assigned and sent into the heart of the troubles, living in the same houses as the IRA soldiers he's fighting against.

MY NAME IS HARDLY takes the reader on a twenty-year journey through Hardly's life—from the beginning, when he leaves Scotland and joins the Army, to the tragic final days when his time as a spy in Ireland has to come to an end.

What readers are saying about *My Name Is Hardly:*
Martin Crosbie's remarkable storytelling talent is apparent throughout his most recent novel, "My Name Is Hardly." The story seized me from the first paragraph and held me relentlessly until I'd come to the novel's thoughtful and moving conclusion.

Kathleen Lourde (Amazon review)

I have no doubt that when the last piece is in place, Crosbie's work will stand tall as exemplary literary fiction, and a reproach to those who mourn the decline of the "gatekeepers" of commercial publishing. Any gate too small to let in Martin Crosbie should have been blown up a long time ago.

Steven Hart (Goodreads review)

Lies I Never Told—A Collection of Short Stories

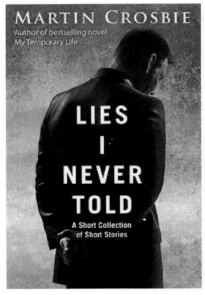

Published April 13, 2013
Publisher—Martin Crosbie
Short Story Collection
Available on Kindle
Amazon US tinyurl.com/q7w7vu3
Amazon UK tinyurl.com/l3ksbky
Amazon Canada tinyurl.com/mvew4r6

"It's what we do. We make our own beds. We become thirty and then forty and we divorce and re-marry and visit our children on weekends, and work at jobs we never dreamed of doing, and have too many relationships with people we don't like, and on the outside we look like any other forty-year-old hero. We're not though, because it never goes away. No matter how hard we try to hide it, inside we're still seventeen, sitting at the river, looking for the girl with the brown eyes."

In this collection of short stories, Martin Crosbie, the bestselling author of My Temporary Life, *presents us with a glimpse into the rear-view mirror of life. Crosbie's writing is quiet, so quiet that when the crash comes you suddenly realize you've been gripping onto the edge of your chair, living the story right along with the main character. In this intensely personal collection, he writes about relationships, sex, children, infidelities, guilt, and sometimes, the absence of guilt.*

Lies I Never Told *includes four new, original stories, one previously published short story, and the first chapters of his*

Amazon bestselling novel My Temporary Life *and the follow-up* My Name Is Hardly.

What readers are saying about *Lies I Never Told—A Collection of Short Stories:*
Could not put this book down. I am amazed at the depth of feeling and emotion in his words. All of the stories are so different yet so connected at the emotional level. My only disappointment is that the stories were not longer. I really hope that this book is just a prelude of the novels to come. Martin grabs me from the first line and takes me on an emotional journey with all his characters.

Debbie Dore (Amazon review)

Where Martin Crosbie found his voice is a mystery. His ability to create stories (here very brief ones) that explore the psyche of his chosen stand-in trope in such a way that within a few sentences you are so aware of the character's life and feelings that he seems to be sitting beside you, in conversation with only you.

Grady Harp (Hall of Fame reviewer)—Goodreads review

How I Sold 30,000 eBooks on Amazon's Kindle-An Easy-To-Follow Self-Publishing Guidebook

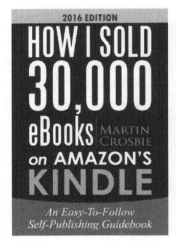

First Published Sept. 4, 2013
Revised 2014, 2015, 2016.
Publisher—Martin Crosbie
Self-Help-Sales and Marketing
Amazon US **tinyurl.com/ppxud2p**
Amazon UK **tinyurl.com/ne7jnmc**
Amazon Canada **tinyurl.com/ozf24m3**

- ✓ Outlines the methods that the top 5% of successful self-published authors utilize to produce their eBooks in a professional, cost-effective manner
- ✓ Shows what happened after Amazon changed the rules and what you need to do right now to adjust your strategy
- ✓ How to adopt the philosophy that will allow promotional opportunities to come to you
- ✓ What you need to know in order to position yourself for a run at the bestseller lists

In February 2012 Martin Crosbie's self-published eBook *My Temporary Life* hit Amazon's top ten overall bestseller list. The next month Amazon posted a press release revealing that Crosbie had made $46,000 in one month, with one book. Previously to this, his novel was rejected one hundred and thirty times by traditional publishers and agents.

In the months that followed, *My Temporary Life* and its sequel have been consistent sellers, often sitting atop Amazon's rankings. Crosbie's story has been mentioned in *Publisher's Weekly*, *Forbes* online, and other media outlets around the world. In fact, Amazon referred to him as one of their 2012 success stories in their year-end press release.

How I Sold 30,000 eBooks on Amazon's Kindle—An Easy-To-Follow Self-Publishing Guidebook tells the story of how he became a full-time writer, detailing the specific steps he took to find and connect with his readers. Plus, it describes how to adjust and tweak your strategy as Amazon changes their systems.

What readers are saying about *How I Sold 30,000 eBooks on Amazon's Kindle-An Easy-To-Follow Self-Publishing Guidebook:*

Yes, I was skeptical because I've read one or two of these books, and their suggestions are... let's just say not that good.

Last night, I skipped the intro and jumped right to the meat of the book. Chapter One was better, much better, than I had expected. But it was when he said, DON'T go out on Twitter and FB and shout "read my book" a thousand times a day that he convinced me that he was honest and knew what he was talking about.

For anyone at the publishing stage or who wants to get there, so far :-) [I will always be a hardcore skeptic] this is a good reference on what to do, on how to build relationships instead of walls. If you're not yet at the publishing stage, start now to build an audience and support group. And Martin C practices what he preaches, especially the part about supporting other authors. He followed me back on Twitter and friended me on FB.

NSW (Amazon Review)

If you are a new writer this book is a must. I wish I had it when I first started writing. It is filled with easy to read and easy to understand information. However, even if you are an already published writer this book will offer you new information you might not have known. I found it helpful in so many ways. There are also links to various other sites that offer valuable info that is very difficult to find. Basically, "How I Sold 30,000 Ebooks on Amazon Kindle," takes a lot of the guessing and hard work out of self publishing.

Roberta Kagan (Amazon Review)

Believing Again: A Tale of Two Christmases

Published Nov. 29, 2013
Publisher—Martin Crosbie
Contemporary/Holiday Romance
Amazon US tinyurl.com/oldbply
Amazon UK tinyurl.com/o2wuc97
Amazon Canada tinyurl.com/njfrxvy

Two weeks before Christmas, Becky gets what she always wanted. James proposes to her and promises that they'll have lots of Christmases together.

When Stephen returns home after serving overseas all he wants is to spend Christmas with his new wife, Myra. All he can think about is her touch, her warmth.

A compelling story of two couples, traveling their separate paths, building their lives together, until one day a secret is revealed that changes all of their lives. And, afterward, nothing will ever be the same again.

Believing Again: A Tale of Two Christmases is a heartwarming tale of love, commitment, family, and, of course, Christmas.

What readers are saying about *Believing Again: A Tale of Two Christmases*:
Simply put, "Believing Again: A Tale of Two Christmases" is the best Christmas themed novel I have read in a long, long, long time. Martin Crosbie is an enchanting story teller. This is a story that sticks in the mind and heart; I know it will stick in mine for a long time.

G. Polley (Goodreads Review)

Believing Again is an amazing story - a slice of life which reminds you of the fragility of the human spirit and the resiliency of love. Martin's novel lets us follow two couples as they make their journey from love to heartache. We see the tales against the backdrop of the holidays which is always a time when life seems to weigh heaviest on our hearts. Believing Again is poignant and bittersweet, not a traditional romance, but a realistic look at love and loss and the hope that despite the valleys in our path, we should never give up the dream that we can find true love if we keep our minds and our hearts open to the possibility.

Lillibet (Amazon Review)

Please connect with me:

https://twitter.com/Martinthewriter

https://www.facebook.com/martin.crosbie.3

martincrosbie.com/

martin@martincrosbie.com

Made in the USA
San Bernardino, CA
01 June 2018